TRESPASSING:
Houses x Artists

With essays by

Alan Koch and Linda Taalman, OpenOffice
Cara Mullio
L.D. Riehle

Edited by

Bellevue Art Museum
in collaboration with the MAK Center for Art and Architecture, L.A.

Hatje Cantz Publishers

This book was published on the occasion of the exhibition *TRESPASSING: Houses x Artists*
at the Bellevue Art Museum and MAK Center for Art and Architecture, L.A.

Exhibition: Cara Mullio, OpenOffice, Kathleen Harleman and Ginger Gregg Duggan/Bellevue Art Museum
Curator (Bellevue Art Museum): Cara Mullio
Curator (MAK Center for Art and Architecture): LouAnne Greenwald
Project Manager (MAK Center for Art and Architecture): Martina Kandeler-Fritsch
Project Coordinator (MAK Center for Art and Architecture): Gamynne Guillotte

Bellevue Art Museum, Bellevue, Washington
August 31, 2002–January 5, 2003
MAK Center for Art and Architecture, L.A., West Hollywood, California
January 29–July 27, 2003
MAK Vienna, 2003

This publication is made possible in part by the Federal Ministry of Education, Science
and Culture and Federal Chancellery, Department for the Arts of the Republic of Austria;
the National Endowment for the Arts; City of Los Angeles, Cultural Affairs Department;
City of West Hollywood; LLWW Foundation; and the New York Foundation for the Arts.

NATIONAL
ENDOWMENT
FOR THE ARTS

Editor: Bellevue Art Museum in collaboration with the MAK Center for Art and Architecture, L.A.
Catalogue Editing: Stephanie Emerson
Copyediting: Stephanie Emerson
Graphic Design: Michael Worthington
Type Design: Pete Bergeron

Bellevue Art Museum
510 Bellevue Way NE, Bellevue, WA 98004, U.S.A.
Tel. (+1-425) 519 0770, Fax (+1-425) 637 1799
www.bellevueart.org

MAK Center for Art and Architecture, L.A.
835 North Kings Road, West Hollywood, CA 90069, U.S.A.
Tel. (+1-323) 651 1510, Fax (+1-323) 651 2340
www.MAKcenter.com

Published by
Hatje Cantz Publishers
Senefelderstrasse 12, 73760 Ostfildern-Ruit, Germany
Tel. (+49-711) 4405-0, Fax (+49-711) 4405-220
www.hatjecantz.de

Distribution in the US:
DAP/Distributed Art Publishers, Inc.
155 Avenues of the Americas, second floor, New York, NY 10013
Phone (+1-212) 627 1999, Fax (+1-212) 627 9484

ISBN 3-7757-1261-5
Printed in Germany by Cantz

Contents

Foreword
Kathleen Harleman
Peter Noever

·TRESPASSING: Houses x Artists (read "houses by artists") has the dynamic of creative collaboration at its core. In 1998, architects Alan Koch and Linda Taalman initiated the TRESPASSING: Houses x Artists project as a forum in which to engage a wide range of artists in dialogue about the design of houses. Through this initiative, Koch and Taalman founded the New York-based practice of OpenOffice as a platform for art and architecture collaborations. A partnership with the MAK Center for Art and Architecture, L.A., transformed TRESPASSING into a comprehensive exhibition and catalogue. Nine contemporary artists were each asked to design a house under optimal creative conditions in an ideal creative setting. Participating artists include: Kevin Appel, Barbara Bloom, Chris Burden, Jim Isermann, T. Kelly Mason, Julian Opie, Renée Petropoulos, David Reed, and Jessica Stockholder. Their works have been constructed for installation in a museum setting, and documented and explored in the accompanying catalogue. Unrestricted by the external demands of program, scale, site condition, finances, and architectural preconceptions, the artists were able to consider the house in absolute terms as a spatial and social hypothesis.

Each artist was invited to propose a house concept in any terms important to their investigations, with the single requirement that their ideas could be mediated into an architectural proposal in collaboration with OpenOffice. Proceeding from the notion of a project without a client, the artists' ideas transformed shifting desires and values of our changing cultural consciousness. Extending their investigations beyond the formal sculptural properties of a model they have proposed radical solutions to the basic idea of shelter and human behavior.

This unprecedented collaborative undertaking transgresses the spatial relationship between art and architecture, obviating the distinctions between them. What emerges is an organic integration of skin and substance, an expanded spatial ecology.

Historically, the house has been a testing ground for new building technologies and social paradigms. It is also the architectural form to which people attach their deepest aesthetic, psychological, and physiological impulses about built spaces. In an era of diminishing privacy and fluid social patterns, modes of contemporary living require creative reimaginings. TRESPASSING incorporates research, investigation, and re-conceptualizations that are open to questioning the physical or social manifestations of domestic life. This exhibition brings together artists, architects, curators, and the public to explore new materials and ideas about the nature, function, and form of the house. Developed in close association with Alan Koch and Linda Taalman of OpenOffice and curator, Cara Mullio, the artists' projects are presented as architectural models, partial realizations, and digital works using computer graphics, and virtual software.

The power of the individual artists' projects is great, as are the opportunities to present them as interventions in resonant and strong architectural environments—R.M. Schindler's Kings Road House, now the MAK Center, in Los Angeles, California and Steven Holl's Bellevue Museum of Art, in Bellevue, Washington. The nine contemporary artists whose projects are featured trespass the discipline of architecture.

SPECULATION AND COMMUNICATION
ALAN KOCH AND LINDA TAALMAN

Speculation and Communication
A Conversation Between
Alan Koch and Linda Taalman, OpenOffice

Robert Irwin, diagram of "Art as a Discipline"

ALAN KOCH: Why the house?

LINDA TAALMAN: The house is something that everybody fixates on to some degree — everyone knows a particular house, has lived in a house, has an experience of being in a house, has dreams of a house and ideas of a house.

AK: In our invitation we said that the house is the one thing you can ask just about anybody to try to think about in formal terms. With a house they can go into real detail because its something that most people have spent a lot of time fantasizing about.

As a vehicle to study how to make things with other people such as artists, the more open-ended the structure, the more that people can think about it on their own; then the more rich the public participation in the results of the project can be. Because the public can already think about a house formally on their own, they're going to have a deeper level of insight when they look at our two disciplines creating the houses together.

LT: Houses evolve very much on their own through the inhabitants who modify them and create trends within neighborhoods or desires on an even larger scale. The *TRESPASSING: Houses x Artists* project is exploring speculation as a process. In addition to new ideas of houses, this project brings up an idea of practice through speculation — an idea of being your own catalyst, of finding a way to generate projects and ideas without having to fit within an already institutionalized process.

AK: This is crucial to OpenOffice's practice in specific and important to architecture in general. As architects we're confronted with the problem that, for us, the client comes first and the artifact comes second. Which means the client is a mechanism of production. You need that mechanism to be in place before you actually begin the production. That's especially frustrating as a young office. And so we looked to artists. For artists it tends to work in the opposite direction. The artifact is produced first and then the owner discovers it in a completed state. This is a potentially powerful model for architects, but one that requires new devises being applied to the traditional mechanisms of production.

LT: The word "speculative" means different things — there is the idea of the speculative house or the "spec" house. A spec house is a developer's idea where you make a house and then try to sell it to different owners who might be interested. Being the architect or the creator as opposed to a developer — to be from the point of zero capital and to propel the idea — is a different model of freedom. Schindler tried to work with a similar method of speculation, designing and building houses — including the purchase of land.

There is also a tradition of speculative, experimental architecture that influenced our desire to do something other than just provide a service for clients. Many architects have produced houses speculatively either as only drawings or as buildings in order to create an interest in their work. But that has normally been an entirely solitary practice. We

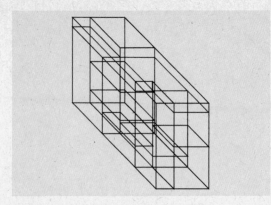

Julian Opie, early house proposal diagram

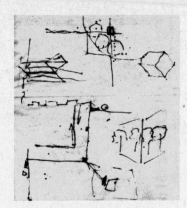

Kevin Appel, early house proposal diagram

were not interested in simply developing a language strictly of our own and then applying it to different scales and projects as other clients come along later.

We set out to build a practice by engaging other practicioners, and from developing house concepts we expected to move into different discussions of explorations. We planned to start with this very pure form of architecture, the house, which is rudimentary, and we wanted to expand on that. We wanted to create a language of dialogue around the subject of the house.

AK: What does the group dynamic have beyond the solitary? Does it actually make the project more viable? Is it more likely to have real impact in a building culture?

LT: The group dynamic brings another dimension. One project being worked on by multiple hands makes that project into more of a communication instead of a language of pure form. We wanted to direct the investigation into a space where it's out of our control and into a space of discussion. Not being in total control broadens the process and invites other points of view, which may have a greater impact on the public. By having a broadened point of view, more people are able to access the idea and plug in their own ideas for future development.

Robert Irwin has a diagram, describing the spheres of operation that he posits as a potential understanding of the artistic discipline and its relationship to the outside world. As opposed to a hierarchical model the diagram represents a collective of actions needed to make a discipline of art into meaningful social action.

This parallels our own intent to crack open the practice of architecture to a broadened scope and question the discipline and the potential roles of the architect. A key feature predicated in the non-hierarchical order of Irwin's diagram allows for one to start anywhere along the axis of motive. We started in an engagement with creative colleagues, in a space of dialog and speculation where we could suspend our disbelief. In its realization this project serves to stimulate pure inquiry in the artists'/architects' studio, tectonic and material invention and re-engineering, question representation thru exhibition, and eventually a potential building.

AK: And legibility is important...

LT: That's the communication. The project has to constantly explain itself and make itself clear, so that the other parties involved can understand what the discussion is about and where it's going and where it's coming from.

AK: What is good about the structure of the dialogue is that there's a dynamic that makes the work happen. On the generative side, the curiosity between the disciplines is creating a dynamic of motion, of probing and reacting. And on the viewing side, all those curiosities become lenses from which you can look into the results.

T. *Kelly Mason, early house proposal sketch*

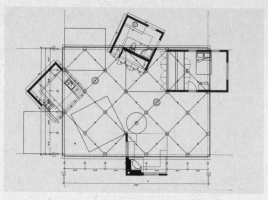

T. *Kelly Mason, plan with one bedroom, kitchen, bath, and living room*

LT: Two models for the project that we began with were the idea of building expositions and the pattern books that originate from treatises of architectural order developed by architects and planners all the way back to Vetruvius and the *Ten Books on Architecture*.

The pattern book has been greatly down-scaled in terms of an idea. Now pattern books are only seen in supermarkets or the shelter magazines and their content is completely removed from the architectural practice and has become the developer's realm.

AK: There are two other models. One is architectural—the California Case Study. This was primarily a magazine venue for showing off new ideas about technology—postwar technology primarily—and architecture. And out of that public design discussion came a few houses modeled [on] those ideas, and ultimately, through publication, had a profound effect on the suburban West Coast where those models were taken seriously and found their way into the popular consciousness locally and on the architectural consciousness globally.

Another model is the concept car, in which experimental cars are produced that they know can't go into production for limitations of one reason or another. But those concept cars play a big role in the future waves of cars that will actually be produced; those ideas are percolating in the public and the industry where the demands are being created.

LT: In the light of these models, the role of the project's relationship to the public became pivotal; the idea of doing an exhibition of this project is to present ideas to the public in a diverse and accessible range of media. By engaging people through different scales and materials and using all of the sensory tools, this multilayered engagement creates an open space for people interacting with the ideas. It's about presenting the communication in a fun way so that a broad audience can engage it without it being strictly intellectual.

AK: Has the exhibition become a surrogate for what architects usually start with, which is a site, a specific site on which to respond to a program? Given the lack of a real space, how do you formalize a bunch of ideas about a house that are not rooted to a neighborhood or a climate or a natural feature?

LT: The exhibition is not exclusively a surrogate site; it's a site that the project takes place in and [is] installed in. The site as an architectural dilemma is in a kind of crisis. In this project there is a crisis because it's not evident where the house "is." Many of the projects have had to internalize this idea of site. And that internalization is either through creating its own artificial landscape, like in Jessica Stockholder's house, where it has a site creation around itself, or other adaptable or modular ideas, like T. Kelly Mason's, which can go to many different places and the site is literally the space created by the dweller through their individualistic organization of a kit of parts.

AK: Are the houses being influenced by the fact that they are to be exhibited as proposal[s] for houses

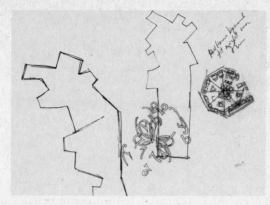 

Renée Petropoulos, plan studies　　　　　*Jessica Stockholder, sketch of house with site*

versus as if they were to be just built as houses?

LT: There's a relationship between this plan of presenting the ideas of the house in a mediated fashion through exhibition and book and the problem of a non-site. There's a link between those two things that allows them to deal with these two different elements of the process.

AK: A problem of architecture is that representation is the basis of the decision making process—from design decisions to client approvals. Therefore, it follows that what is ultimately realized as built structures is that which best lends itself to representation (client presentation).

　　　In an exhibition you're trying to convince people about ideas by representing them through that format. The exhibition is able to focus on the dialogue and therefore the ideas that formulate the making of the houses. And the visuality of the artists lent to the drawings, films, and models of the houses have deeper interpretations than would traditional architectural presentations the public has come to expect.

LT: Another important concept in this project is about the programming of a house. The house as an architectural model or an architectural type has certain stable definitions and certain constantly changing definitions. And part of the interest in doing this project is to define what the program of a house is now.

　　　A need for intensified specificity and flexibility has been addressed by all of the artists' houses in the programming. It's either been addressed as architecture programmed with specific tendencies or as an idea of a flexible model. And that goes back to this idea of site. The need for specificity or flexibility and the need for customizability or options are an expression of a desired freedom and user friendliness.

AK: The reason that flexible systems are designed is because there's no one to customize it to, even though there's a desire to provide specificity. So one provides vehicles through which an end user can find customizing as an option. The artists' houses are also responding to the lack of specifics by either taking advantage of the lack or trying to replace it by creating their own system for being adaptable.

LT: Given the absence of the user, the solutions in the houses that we've come up with are extremes. All have the idea of system or model of architecture or a domestic option and have a highly designed and customized or pre-defined environment that you can adapt or be adapted to after you move in. It's a question of where the adaptation is.

　　　These are two different ways of approaching the dilemma of adaptation or inhabitation and there are combinations of the two. All of the projects may have a little bit of both. We're allowing totally non-hierarchical definitions of domestic space. We're trying to engage a set of sociological and cultural rules and views that are out there, ideas that are in architecture and in a way are anti-architectural.

Artistic Process
A Conversation between Alan Koch,
Linda Taalman, and Rodney Hill

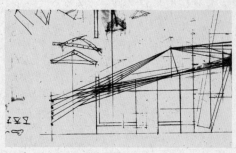

Jessica Stockholder, roof study

AK: Why artists? We've always said that we looked for artists that were working with architectural ideas but that hadn't really resolved them in their work in terms of production. It was more that they were obliquely intersecting architecture.

LT: Is that because their work wasn't visibly a building? Because I think you could say that Jessica Stockholder's work is architectural, but it's not a building.

AK: There's a leap between things that are accomplished through one's own hands, or are not really about planning but more about reacting and the process of representing what one wants to accomplish. I would say Jessica, for example, has a strategy where she'll plan to a certain level and then she knows that she doesn't want to think abstractly all the way to the end.

Another thing that's important here is that architects are always working with the problem of representation. As an architect, you plan and you need to sell your idea visually as a representation of what you're going to do, whereas an artist can make a whole string of works and then doesn't need to represent what they're going to be like. As architects it's interesting to get involved with people that work with the idea of representation directly.

LT: The model we're making for Julian Opie is not a true representation of his house. It's a version of the house at a smaller scale, built with materials that have to be resolved at that scale. There are aspects of representation that are being questioned because we're physically working with media and material, but as a representation of a building it's very different because it's not completely realized as a miniature version, it's a thing itself.

AK: A similar question is raised with Chris Burden's small skyscraper as it's going to be represented as a small, small skyscraper of a small skyscraper. And the small, small skyscraper is made out of the same technology, just a reduced size with the same connection details and everything.

RODNEY HILL: Do you find that architectural ideas normally get bogged down by the practicalities of realizing a building? Do you have to discard an idea because you already know that rainwater is going to have this or that negative effect? Is taking an idea that an artist proposes confronting you to accommodate for a more challenging realization?

AK: We are trying to get beyond our preconceptions and not just assume the things that you would if you're working in a strictly logical system about rainwater or other dilemmas of shelter.

LT: Trying to just make an architectural idea become a functional building is usually ninety percent of the job. But here we are open to the possibility that the rainwater issue, that the building is leaking, is of an utmost importance as opposed to just a backburner thing that has to be resolved. For example, in David Reed's house there are now places where we want the roof to leak.

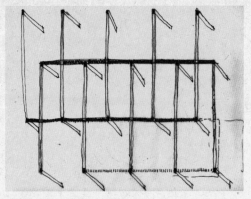

Jim Isermann, sketch of structural/drainage system

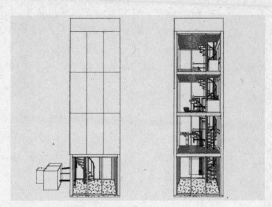

Chris Burden, elevations of small skyscraper

AK: And Jim Isermann's roof presents the main architectural form and the main problem as well. It has valleys that have no escape except through structural members. And so being presented with a roof that doesn't drain normally becomes integral to the idea of the house. Or how light is filtered, the light in the house is directed through the roof, as its folded forms rest on top of the glazed brick walls, creating the unique clerestory condition that is essential to Jim's vision of the project. The bright safety yellow roof becomes a glowing cap for the entire house, and object within its environment, as well as a filter for resisting and admitting the exterior elements.

LT: It's also important to talk about Jessica's house, in this discussion of roofs. Her first critique of the architectural model we generated from her drawings was that our model was so slick. We had the first preconceived architectural reaction in the whole project right there in that model. Where she had a pitched roof concept we made it a lean-to; architects have an impossible relationship with the pitched roof formally, as this more traditional roof seems anti-architectural. And she envisioned this pitched roof as emblematic of its house-ness. That was really a hurdle to get over. From that point on I became interested in looking at the pitched roof as a new kind of idea.

RH: In talking about anti-architecture, were you hoping to be helped into being able to embrace anti-architecture for yourself?

LT: The original idea was not that the project would be anti-architectural. We thought that artists would be focused on different necessities of architecture, what architecture actually provides—different kinds of programs or a different reasoning for making decisions, not necessarily for making anti-architectural ideas. I think that just came out of it naturally.

RH: So if you're taking art and architecture and hybridizing them, is the goal to make the domestic perform both functionally in an architectural realm as well as in the sculptural realm? Is it that you might live in a giant sculpture and/or in art, as the bond between sculpture and architecture?

LT: Recent architecture designed by cutting edge architects is much more like living in theatrical sculptures than what we're doing. In many instances we are dealing with more base, pragmatic issues, taking them on as the primary architecture as opposed to secondary decisions. With T. Kelly Mason, for example, the house is comprised of prefabricated building technologies mixed with other industrial technologies and these become the two main determinants of the house. Roto-molded plastic modules, ribbed for structural integrity, function with a cladded sheet-metal and glass building enclosure and a steel shed structure. The house is made easy to create, easy to build, easy to make as an assembly-line product. Work with what's known, work with what's out there, and make it cheap and widely accessible.

Chris Burden, drawing collage of small skyscraper plans and elevations

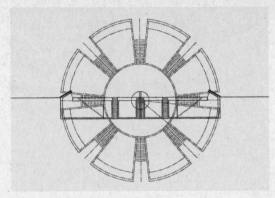

Barbara Bloom, plan/section study

RH: I think Chris Burden was an interesting choice because he seems to be all about pushing things to their limit. So I think it was a courageous choice on your part in a way to choose someone who might produce a house that is physically demanding. Of course, he pushed the law instead.

AK: It turns out he's pushing engineering to the limit, too. We're looking at building with a modular aluminum extrusion system that's used to make jewelry display cases and clean rooms and work-benches. Constructing a house out this material has never been done; it's like building an extra-large model, and the small model is really just a smaller version of the actual building.

LT: The idea is also that it's within reach [because] the material's lightweight—you can actually carry it up to your site by yourself. Or as Chris says, "with a friend and a donkey." It's a do-it-yourself idea. And this continues the idea of doing it without permission.

AK: Chris is the only example of a house that existed as a pretty highly finalized idea before *TRESPASSING* started. And since then he's taken the opportunity to take it to the next level.

RH: Has Barbara Bloom's project become grounded yet?

LT: The project concept is grounded but it has a different goal as a project. The idea of her house is all about staying afloat.

AK: When we started, the only idea we imposed was that the house would be buildable. And through the process, especially in working with Barbara, we realized that wasn't a tenable guideline any more.

RH: She got hers suspended out of buildable?

AK: Yes. She ultimately convinced us that buildable is only interesting for people that want to build. But it's not interesting for others that are just thinking about the house. For Barbara, it's more of an instrument to look through to see a house or to think about your existing house. Furniture and surfaces take on architectural dimensions through variable colors, textures, and materials that can be changed at will. Redecorating wishes such as "discard all pink items" or "move all round shapes" can be swiftly executed. It's a lens more than a house; it's a game to divine the way things are organized or classified in the normal house.

LT: The initial premise of how *TRESPASSING* would work and what the interesting things about it would be has changed over the course of the project. Originally we thought the house proposals would be ready-made ideas that could be presented to the public as viable building options. Now the project's not necessarily about the houses being buildable. It's also about thinking about houses and how you relate to them. And how can you think about them differently? Can we uncover what's been over-looked or forgotten?

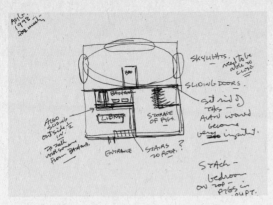

David Reed, sketch for house proposal

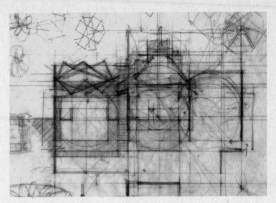

David Reed, roof studies

AK: My perspective of the project has changed significantly since we began. When it started it was much more of a system that would be self-fulfilling and the proposals would just change slightly because of the different collaborators. Our input, even though we're throughout all the projects, is also very different in each house, partially because we worked with each artist separately to develop a process that was particular to the way they were working and not just trying to do a cookie cutter.

LT: It's possible that you could expand on the process that we're now using for finalizing the designs of the houses. For example, with David Reed we're going to develop totally different architectures within the same house—industrial concrete panels, corrugated metal and fiberglass, plywood, sliding glass doors, counterweighted floor, drawn curtains, roving beds, storage units—and allow for them to co-exist and possibly be changed up until the last second. The space only exists with the momentary placement of transportable building materials. In the building of the house we would also have to allow for that, so the house could continually change.

This idea of mutability, of a perpetually mutable design process, is developing in many of the house proposals. This is certainly true with Renée Petropoulos's project. Her house came to a point where it could only become more and more refined as a building. That was not interesting as a solution to the original program of a multiple family dwelling. So it went back two steps. Now the architecture is based in a system that will allow the house to be

perpetually collaged but not suffer as result, created by collaging assorted forms and programs of a specific type—market awnings, Plexiglas cash windows, graphic signage, raised sidewalks and other minimart elements.

RH: We've talked about the artist as a replacement of the client. By exchanging the client who is very goal-oriented for someone who's actually absolutely willing to constantly question the whole process and then turn it around at the last moment and look at it upside down again just before making a commitment, you've made a very tall order for yourself to work with clients in this way.

LT: It seems contradictory to what architects need to do in order to sustain themselves because they're dependent upon the efficiency and scale of the project for their own survival. But if projects could be suspended in this way until the resolution is uncovered it would yield a better material reality. At the end of the dialogue between architect and client you might decide that you actually don't need to change anything and you really just need to make all the lightbulbs a different type. Or maybe you just need to change the way that you move through the house.

RH: At some point in the process did each of the houses undergo a radical transformation?

LT: To some degree they have all had a catharsis at one moment or another. For example, David

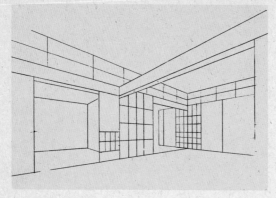

Kevin Appel, perspective sketch

Reed's house has changed radically from its original architectural proposal, which at one point was completely resolved. The premise set out with very achievable goals, but the architectural resolutions did not allow for the kind of chance or idiosyncrasy that was desired. The house concept is still a bedroom/gallery but the architectural references have shifted from the very pristine model of a Guarino Guarini dome, with strict geometry, to other vernacular architectures or imaginary architectures that allow for such architectural ideas as a "ruin" to be realized.

There's an unfixedness to all the projects. With Kevin Appel, for example, we're now trying to work with the idea of a real site. The form's not locked in, but we're working to make the ideas react to the specific qualities of the site, assembling the architectural ideas around it. But the ideas are not restrictive. You can go to a different site and think about the same concepts. How does the space relate to the garden? How does the view through the house and the garden create that same tension?

RH: When the house was in its site-less state it seemed like the designs on paper were for a house that could be perfect anywhere. Could the house exist successfully in a number of places?

AK: Kevin's house could be more a strategic reaction to *site* and *sight*, in a way, and less of a singular structure. He realizes that it's not all formally resolvable until there are absolute limits that only the particularities of an actual commission can bestow. Until then, he has this vision of glass volumes that people are floating within and no place for a kitchen—for example—as we know it.

LT: Kevin is continually stripping the house back, removing the structure that we keep putting in, in favor of a pure view through frameless glass windows and bringing it back into this world of floating planes where transparency mixes with translucency. So that's the problem: How do you make a house that's like a series of floating planes? Where the roof appears to hover and you're never really sure if you're inside or outside and you don't have a kitchen island and range in your way?

AK: You have to redefine the kitchen to make it fit in that vision of the house.

LT: And maybe this way of life is extreme, he's insisting on a way of living through looking. All the artist's houses are asking: does way of life have to be re-addressed?

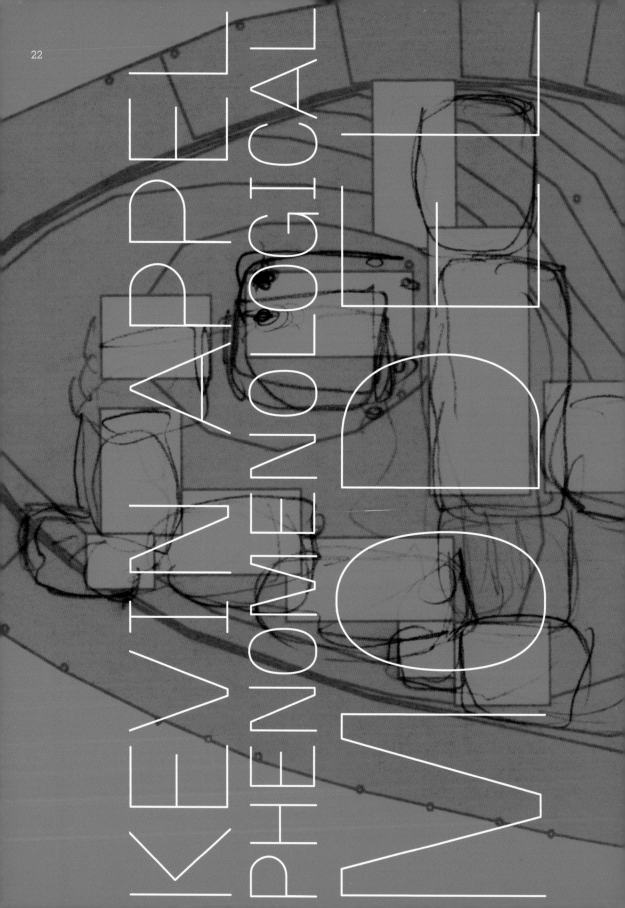

KEVIN APPEL

PHENOMENOLOGICAL

MODEL

Kevin Appel's proposal—a glass house in a garden—generates
and elevates sensory and aesthetic experiences. Transparency and
translucency mesh architecture and landscape to create unlimited
visual freedom and openness while isolating and exposing the body
in space. Domestic privacy and comfort are sublimated to the gaze.

    A set of semi-detached, interconnected pavilions and gardens
refocus the site onto itself as a series of garden vignettes that
surround and infiltrate glass-enclosed living spaces. The paradox
of a glass house's relationship with nature magnifies with the multi-
plicity of views within views, from glass room to garden to glass room
to garden.

    The glass functions both as a window and barrier, revealing
and dividing the choices necessary for experiencing and inhabiting
the house; glass finishes such as fritted, sandblasted, and tinted/
mirrored surfaces are strategically arranged to shift relations of
communal and solitary, inside to outside, and "here" to "there". All
the rooms are in visual proximity from any given point in the house;
viewed rooms remain unobstructed to the eye but maintain distinct
divisions for the body. This disengagement of the eye from the body
creates the sense of floating in the space between physical and
visual occupation.

    The phenomenology of viewing is given precedence over the
functionality and efficiency of the home, allowing the experiential
qualities—the movement of leaves, the change in natural light, and
the silent ballet of other dwellers—to suspend activities of living in a
perpetual state of visual play.

INTERLOCKING
BOXES COULD
BE FOOTPRINT
AND ELEVATION?

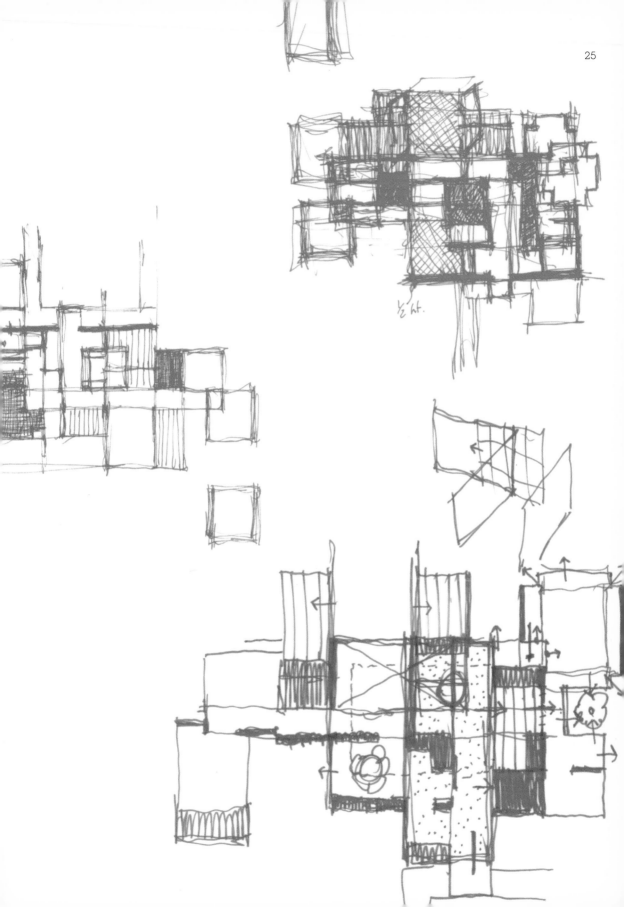

½ ht.

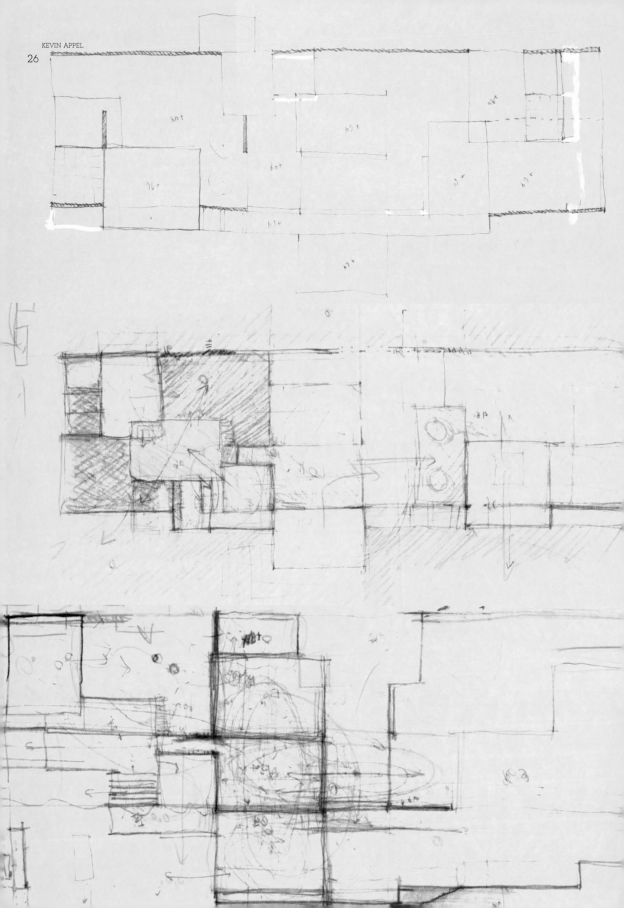

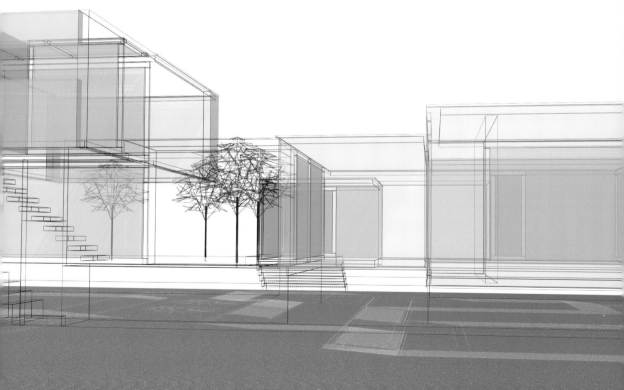

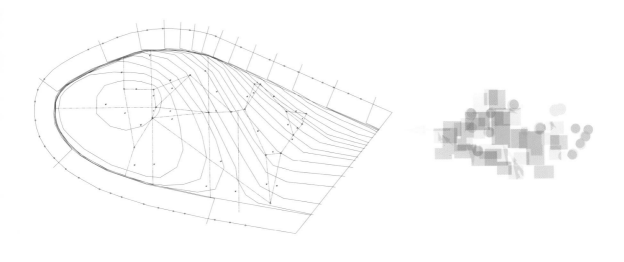

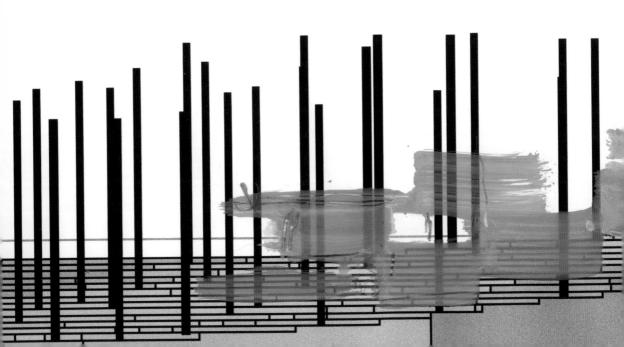

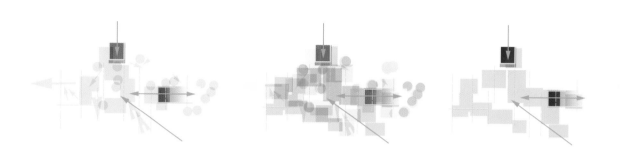

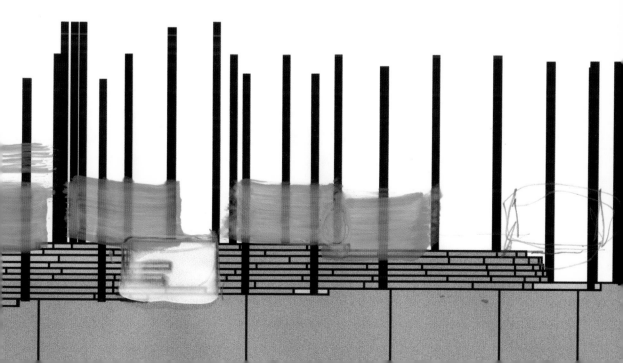

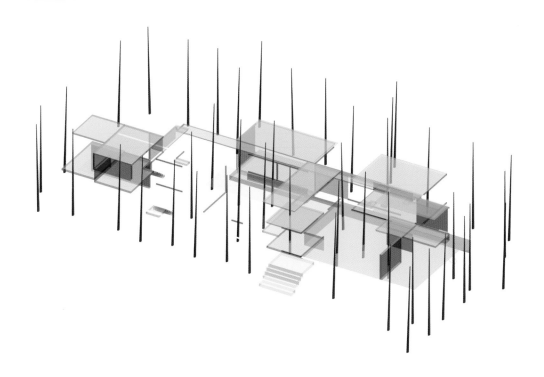

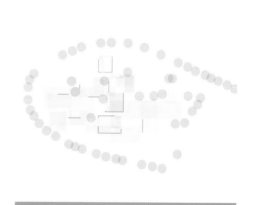

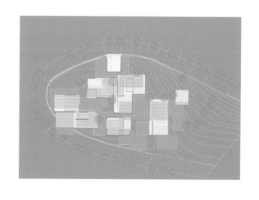

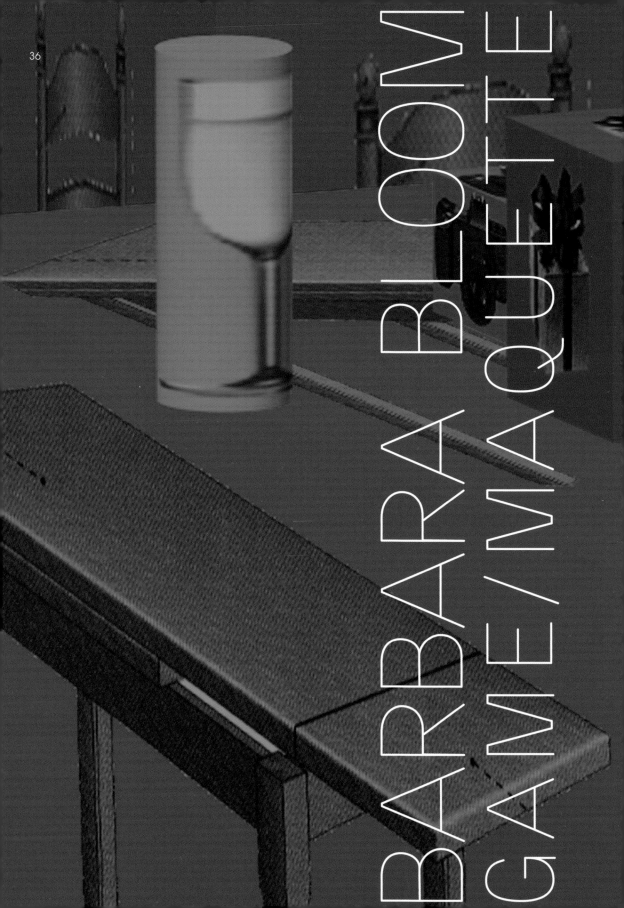

BARBARA BLOOM
GAME/MAQUETTE

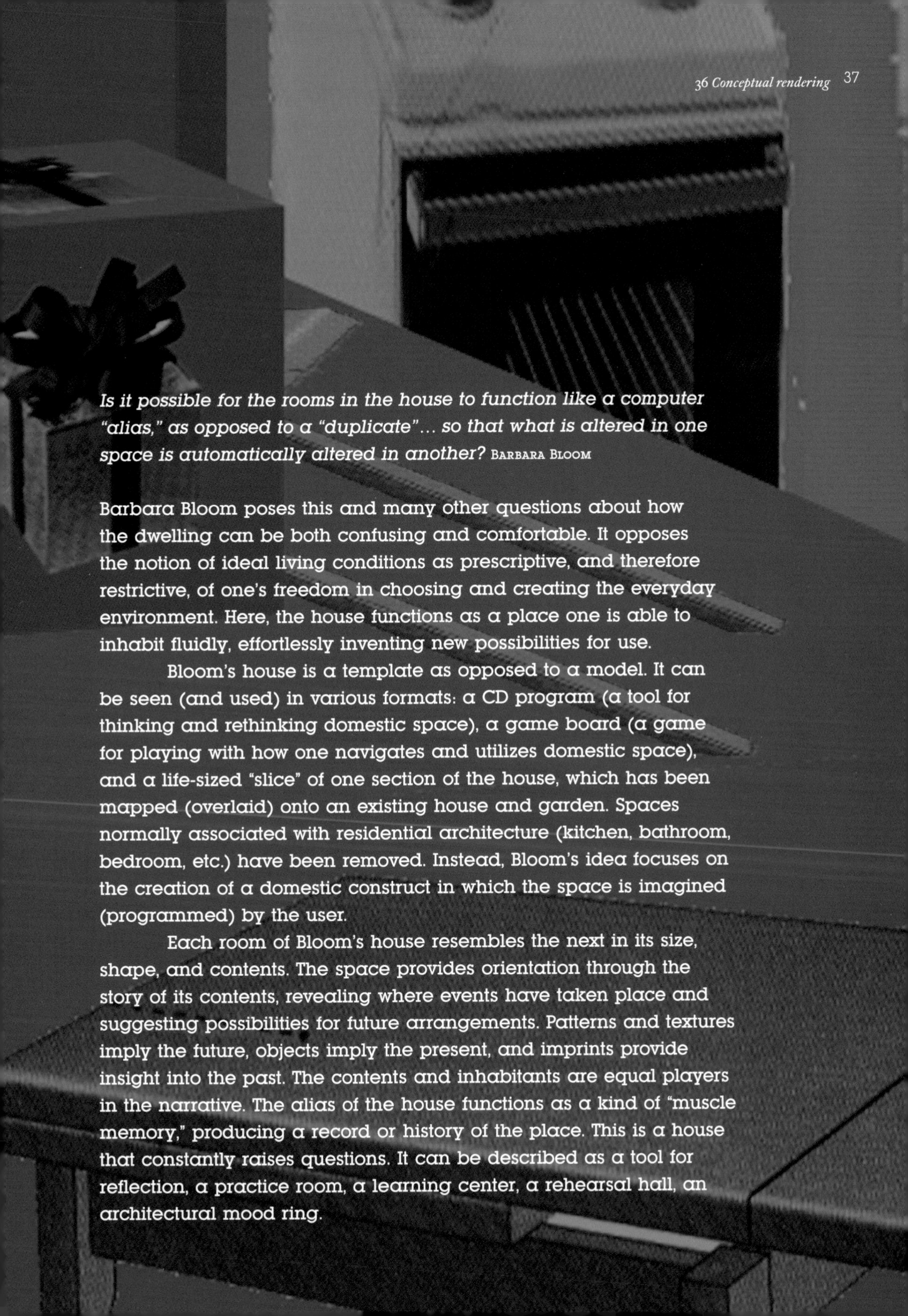

Is it possible for the rooms in the house to function like a computer "alias," as opposed to a "duplicate"… so that what is altered in one space is automatically altered in another? BARBARA BLOOM

Barbara Bloom poses this and many other questions about how the dwelling can be both confusing and comfortable. It opposes the notion of ideal living conditions as prescriptive, and therefore restrictive, of one's freedom in choosing and creating the everyday environment. Here, the house functions as a place one is able to inhabit fluidly, effortlessly inventing new possibilities for use.

Bloom's house is a template as opposed to a model. It can be seen (and used) in various formats: a CD program (a tool for thinking and rethinking domestic space), a game board (a game for playing with how one navigates and utilizes domestic space), and a life-sized "slice" of one section of the house, which has been mapped (overlaid) onto an existing house and garden. Spaces normally associated with residential architecture (kitchen, bathroom, bedroom, etc.) have been removed. Instead, Bloom's idea focuses on the creation of a domestic construct in which the space is imagined (programmed) by the user.

Each room of Bloom's house resembles the next in its size, shape, and contents. The space provides orientation through the story of its contents, revealing where events have taken place and suggesting possibilities for future arrangements. Patterns and textures imply the future, objects imply the present, and imprints provide insight into the past. The contents and inhabitants are equal players in the narrative. The alias of the house functions as a kind of "muscle memory," producing a record or history of the place. This is a house that constantly raises questions. It can be described as a tool for reflection, a practice room, a learning center, a rehearsal hall, an architectural mood ring.

Highrise with staircase
Two versions of house as septagon

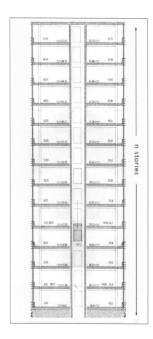

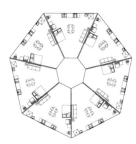

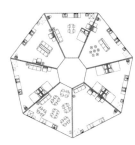

20 QUESTIONS

The following questions and answers are loosely derived from a three-year conversation between Barbara Bloom, Linda Taalman, and Alan Koch.

1. Orientation: Is it bigger than a breadbox?
Or: Animal/vegetable/or mineral?

The first version of the house was based on a number of floors with a single dwelling on each floor. The approach was conceived as an elevator with only one button. By pushing this "random" button one would arrive at an arbitrary floor without knowing which one. Each "house" is a large room containing all the amenities for living — a bed, a table and chairs, a kitchen, a couch, a bathroom, etc. — and is identical to all others. Essential to the project is the tension between a sense of comfort at the prospect of being at home, coupled with never knowing exactly where one is.

Another version has the house on a horizontal plane, a septagonal structure, with seven identical spaces, each accessed by a door at the core of the building. Is the furniture stationary or movable? Can objects move from one house to another?

Other versions have come and gone: game boards with flexible rules, an elevated spinning building, courtyard access with moving gardens, moving sidewalks. Each brought with it particular advantages and problems. Each problem elicited more or less intelligent and elegant design solutions.

I suspect that there is a flaw inherent in trying to decide whether this is an imagined house (one that can defy natural properties of time and space), *or* one that could actually be built. Each version brings with it a different set of problems to be solved. The solutions are what determine what is essential about the house, but also limit its scope. Maybe the imagined and the concrete can exist simultaneously. It can be frustrating to keep the various versions in mind, especially if concentrating on solving design problems. Everything slips around. Maybe the key is not to concentrate on the solutions, but to stay with the questions… with all their ramifications, their spin-off ideas and implied problems. This is a house that talks back, a house that constantly raises questions.

2. Is this a utopian structure?

Is a utopia an imaginary place with a perfect social and political system, an ideal place or state of things? However, the connotation of utopia is of a fantasy bound to fail. The failure lies not only in the realization of utopias, but in their conception and their interaction with others. Any idealized image of how the world could (should) be is, by nature, prescriptive.

Broken *(cracked celadon vase repaired with gold)*, 2000
The Octagon House *(1853)*, *plan view*
The Tip of the Iceberg, *installation view, 1989*

39

I am not convinced that there is any value in conceiving of perfection for oneself and certainly not for others. The house is not a model or an ideal. The house is a tool for reflection. Perhaps a bit like a meditation, it's possibilities become apparent when they are activated by use; it is a practice room.

The Ideal: In the Japanese tradition broken ceramics can be repaired using the *urushi* method. The objects are distinguished by cracks filled with gold, a technique as labor intensive as dental work. In this act damage is not covered up and history is accepted and honored. Value, perfection, and ideal, as we know them are subverted.

3. Is the "house" the building as a whole, or is the "house" each individual unit?

Like a hologram or DNA, each part carries all the information of the whole. It's easy to imagine divisions between the spaces being taken away or the inhabitant could give some or most of the house (rooms) to others. The house can be shared: a commune, a hotel, a compound…

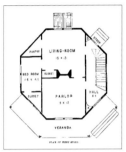

4. So when you misplace your keys, how do you find them?

Since I am an incessant key loser, this is a most interesting question. Do we imagine that there is only one set of my keys? Are there duplicates in all of the spaces so that they are always close at hand? And can we imagine a place where there are not only duplicate, but also aliases?

On a computer there is a distinction between duplicate and alias: A "duplicate" is a copy of something. From the moment the duplicate is created, the original and the duplicate are separate entities. What happens to one does not affect what happens to the other. An "alias" of something is linked to the original. Anything happening to one happens automatically to the other.

If we alter something in one room is an alias of this item altered in another space?

5. Do you refer to your house as science fiction?

I look to science fiction as a place where things are simultaneously familiar and strange, comfortable and disorienting. The house creates a space, which allows you to feel comfortable, and at the same time is a place where you might forget your exact location in space (time). It could be a place where someone could lose track of where (who) one is. Can we conceive a place in which confusion of location is a desirable state? Could the not-knowing exist without the normal accompanying panic or discomfort.

I have indelibly printed in the back of my mind the set for the final scene from *2001: A Space Odyssey*. It has crept into several works of mine and

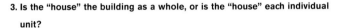

The Reign of Narcissism, *installation view, 1989*
Plan view 'slices' of house

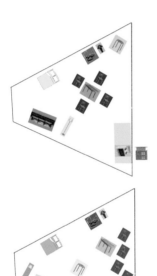

appears here again as a reference point.

Bowman, the surviving astronaut goes on alone… into a world where time and space are relative. He suddenly lands. As his overloaded senses return to normal, he stares aghast out of the pod's window. He's in a room, tranquilly furnished with Louis XVI reproductions (a hotel bedroom suite, a human zoo approximating a hospital). Or rather, he can see himself standing outside the pod, now he is one and the same as the alter ego he sees. He explores the gleaming room with fluorescent floor, all the more alien for its apparent ordinariness. Could it perhaps be an alien idea of what a typical human might want to find at the end of such a journey as this? Some fantasy of luxurious living replicated from an old TV show? Is he a guest or a prisoner? Or perhaps it is an image from Bowman's own mind? Perhaps this is his idea of the perfect place to arrive. It is movingly conventional, as if the most the ill man's imagination can manage in conceiving a better world beyond the infinite is to recollect something he has been taught to see as beautiful in a grand decorating magazine. In the strange, fake room, time jumps and things disappear…

6. How would lost things appear?

Each item—chair, table, toilet, glass, vase, TV, book, etc.—could have a tracking device like a key finder. Ideally, there could be a "finder," a way of calling up any item, but also of dematerializing or transforming items. Keys could be called up and moved to some other place, chairs could be called up and all sent to a certain place, or all dematerialized. And the finder could apply not only to nouns (objects) but adjectives (qualities). So all "red" items could be called up, and moved or turned green. All objects resting on horizontal surfaces could be called up, and the surfaces dematerialized (such that they would appear to be floating).

7. If there were a "finder" in the house what would the criteria, categories, qualities of classifications be?

    surfaces: floor, walls, table, counters
    spatial orientation: height
    vessels
    shape
    material
    color
    sound
    smell
    comfort level: various people ratings
    used by: time
    used by: person (fingerprint recognition)

House icons   41
Chinese language flashcards
House as septagon, with icons

invisible/visible

used for: food/bathing/sitting

most often used/moved

least often used/moved

These categories (qualities) can be determined (programmed) by those who live in the house.

8. If all the rooms of a house are identical, how do you locate yourself in the house?

The Uncertainty Principle discovered by Werner Heisenberg in 1927 showed that in quantum mechanics at a microscopic level, one cannot know both position and velocity with total precision. Moreover, the more precisely you know one, the less precisely you know the other. The Uncertainty Principle tells us that the universe is a frenetic place when examined at smaller and smaller distances and shorter and shorter time scales and that the velocity of electrons severely and unpredictably changes from one moment to the next. And although this was described for electrons, the ideas directly apply to all constituents of nature (both micro-and macroscopic).

    In 1935, the physicist Erwin Schrödinger proposed a "thought exper-iment" to highlight one of the ways in which quantum mechanics contradicts our experiences of reality. His proposal involved placing a cat (a macroscopic object) inside a closed box with a vial of cyanide and a radioactive atom (microscopic object) In the course of one hour the atom could decay, but also, with equal prob-ability, would not. If it decays, then the cyanide is released and the cat dies; if it does not decay, then the cyanide is not released and the cat remains unharmed.

    The paradox arises because the atom, being a microscopic object, must be described by quantum mechanics. After one hour, and before it is observed, the atom is in an equal superposition of being decayed and undecayed. However, if quantum mechanics are a universal and complete theory, then it must describe the whole system. And, since the state of the cat is correlated with the state of the atom, the cat must also be in a superposition of being dead and alive. This clearly contradicts our everyday reality, since we know that the cat in the box is dead, alive, or dying and not in a smeared-out state between the alternatives.

    Only direct observation (opening the box) prevents us from so naively accepting as valid a "blurred model" for representing reality. In itself, it would not embody anything unclear or contradictory.

9. If a house is a machine for living, what kind of machine is it?

Perhaps it is best to make a distinction between a machine and a tool. The machine

窗   window   椅   chair

桌   table   牀   bed

燈   lamp   門   door

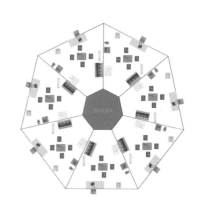

House icons

The Building Blocks of Philosophy from Belief Patterns, *1987*

is expected to do something for you, to provide a function, fulfill a task. A tool is to be used. The house provides an exercise in being comfortable with uncertainty, flexibility, inventiveness. It is an invitation to continually adapt your immediate surroundings to your shifting needs. It is an architectural mood ring.

10. Isn't this like an anonymous hotel room?

Though there are obvious similarities: places where everything one might need to live is available. The international style hotel room is a place where you are not required to make any decisions and a place where the comfort offered is its protection from the outside world.

The house requires constant engagement with the space outside its physical place (What's going on in the rest of the building? The community? The world?). It requires reflection (How am I using the space today?).

11. What activates the dweller to navigate through the house?

Play, restlessness, generosity, need for privacy, need for company, confusion, pleasure, boredom, losing the keys, listening to music, dancing, hunger, sleep…

12. What, if anything, is the prescribed ritual of the inhabitant of the house?

The constant pleasure, responsibility of reassessment and the invention of ways to accommodate change. Change is the constant.

13. What role does spatial memory play in the experience of inhabitation?
  (Do you know where you are by what you have left behind?)

I hope that the design of the house is not just conducive to thinking about spatial memory but to playing with spatial memory. Could surfaces in the house tell you about its past, present, and future?

13. Do you go there to find yourself or lose yourself?

Yes.

> PAST
>
> Marks tell you where you have been:
>
> Footprints on floors
>
> Fingerprints on surfaces
>
> Coffee rings on tables
>
> Wine stains
>
> Lipstick marks on glasses
>
> Faded areas tell where objects have been
>
> Dust tells where nothing has been

PRESENT

Patterns on objects tell you where you are

Everything not in use is grayed out and color patterns tell you what
to use

Carpet pattern

Tile pattern

Wallpaper

Mosaic

Fabric

FUTURE

What tells where you will be?

Windows?

Mirrors?

**14. If utopia and science fiction exist as escapes from reality, how does the
house escape reality – what is its relationship to the everyday?**

This is not a place to escape. It is a place where one's relationship to the world
is heightened through becoming increasingly aware of the everyday choices one
makes. Consciousness of use of space, generosity, greed, desire...

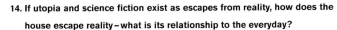

15. How does the house avoid questions of taste and style?

The images have a generic quality. They are not from any particular time. The style
is based on Chinese language flash cards... many come from a visual dictionary,
they are icons. These are the nouns (objects). The way they appear (their style)
could be considered the adjectives. Let's concentrate here on the verbs (their placement, absence, movement, rearrangement, etc.).

16. How does the house situate itself in relation to the outside world?

Can we call it a case house? Maybe it's a leaning center. A rehearsal hall. A practice room.

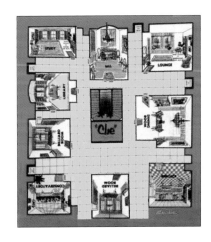

17. Can you travel from room to room?

I originally thought of this house as a building comprised of many stories with a
"random" elevator that would open onto an unknown floor or "house." I have also
considered a single story septagonal structure with a circular conveyor belt that
would encircle an inner courtyard. One would get on a conveyor and get left off
at a (any) door.

      How can we imagine a low-tech mundane transport system "beaming
devise" which gets you from place to place without having to travel through space?

James Lee Byars, TH FI TO IN PH (The First Totally Interrogative Philosophy), *1977*
Saturday Night Live, "The Professional Liar"

Think about the board for the game *Clue*. There you can travel from the "Kitchen" to the "Ballroom" on opposite corners of the board (house) without traversing the board (traveling through the house). Maybe if we saw the house as a maquette, a game in real life scale, that would help. Could it be a maquette for a house in another (parallel) universe? One in which all kinds of movements and properties are possible that we can hardly fathom here?

18. Is the house and answer or a question?

Could each question raised in thinking about the house elicit, as its response, yet another question (and not answers or solutions)?

Couldn't a member of a tribe of colorblind people get the idea of imagining a strange sort of human being (whom we would call "normally sighted")? Couldn't he, for example, portray such a normally sighted person on the stage in the same way as he is able to portray someone who has the gift of prophesy without having it himself?

Would it ever occur to colorblind people to call themselves "colorblind"? Why not?

19. Is this for real? You seem to slide into varying descriptions of this space, depending on what the question is. Are you improvising? Are you making this up as you go along or do you know what you're talking about?

Do you know the "Liar" character on Saturday Night Live? He starts talking and making up a story, and as he hears himself and realizes that something doesn't sound feasible, he covers it by another story (lie) which is itself unbelievable. He, in turn, covers by another lie. It's excruciating in its transparency; his lies are inept and get more and more far fetched.

I like the way that saying one thing causes you to cover with another and another until you are somewhere unintended... out of control... improvised... jazz thinking.

Maybe it is best in thinking about the house to act like the "Liar". Every time one is caught with an inadequate solution, your response would be to up the ante and say, well then, "what if?" and think of a something more far fetched. Don't solve problems... dissolve them.

20. Twenty Questions?

The rules to game of 20 Questions are simple. While one player (the questioner) leaves the room, the others select a word (noun). The questioner returns and has up to twenty questions (to which yes or no can be answered) in which to guess the word.

Imagine a game of 20 Questions in which while the questioner leaves

the room, the others decide to alter the rules, that they will decide on no word at all. Instead, each person will answer yes or no as he pleases, provided the word in his mind fits his own reply and all the previous replies. The questioner returns and, unsuspecting, begins asking questions. The game goes something like this:

Questioner: Is it an animal?

Answerer A: YES. (thinking of DOG)

    All Answerers must change their words to an animal

Questioner: Is it a domestic animal?

Answerer B: NO. (thinking of TIGER)

    Answerer B has changed from FENCE to TIGER

    Answerer A must now change from DOG to LION

Questioner: Does it live on land?

Answerer C: NO. (thinking if SHARK)

    Answerer C has changed from LAMP to HORSE to SHARK

    Answerer B must now change from TIGER to GUPPY

    Answerer A must now change from LION to DOLPHIN

When the questioner begins, he assumes a word already exists, just as physicists beginning an experiment think that reality exists. Yet the word in this game comes into being through the questions raised and the physical world emerges from the observations made. If the player asks different questions, he finds a different word and if scientists perform different experiments they find different realities.

水 water

CHRIS BURDEN

MEDUSA'S HEAD

SKYSCRAPER

46 Topanga Canyon | 48 Small skyscraper, sketch | 49 Small skyscraper, elevation and section
50 Small skyscraper, site A | 51 Small skyscraper, site B | 52 Small skyscraper, site C
53 Small skyscraper, axonometric view | 54 Small skyscraper, site D
55 Small skyscraper, section and connection details

The Los Angeles County Building Code allows small out buildings, i.e., sheds, barns, garages, tool sheds, green houses, etc., under 400 square feet and under thirty-five feet high, to be built without a building permit. Chris Burden

Chris Burden's "small skyscraper" evades Los Angeles building codes by strictly adhering to a literal application of County spatial requirements: each floor measures 100 square feet with a maximum height of thirty-five feet. Advanced lightweight technology allows for an owner to purchase individual structural elements and assemble them without the aid of skilled labor or heavy equipment. The floors of this "self-mountable" house can be arranged as follows: the ground floor entry doubles as living room, the second floor contains the kitchen and provisional dining, the third floor is occupied by the bathroom, and the top floor houses the bedroom. Planned provisional—and "quasi-legal"—spaces include a roof deck at the top and a mechanical/storage basement out of sight below with a secret contemplation space at the very bottom. All services such as water and power are clustered around the vertical shaft of a small, one-person elevator.

Envisioned as a retreat and furnished with modest methods, Burden's dramatically vertical "small skyscraper" requires an intense re-evaluation of the terms of dwelling. Given the legally stipulated maximum floor area of 10' x 10' and the necessity of an elevator, Burden's house dictates an extremely humble occupation of the scant floor area. By applying the formal language of the skyscraper to a modest domestic dwelling, Burden engages questions of power

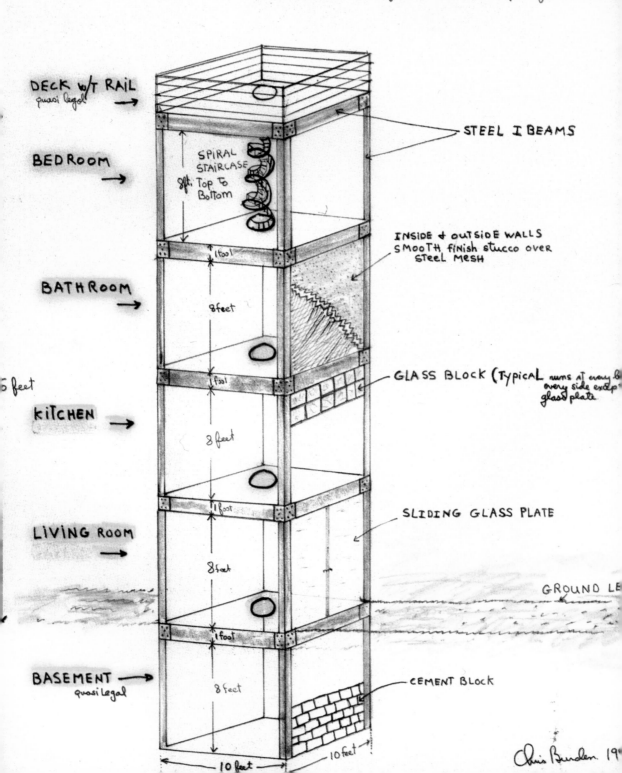

CHRIS BURDEN

48

SMALL SKYSCRAPER 64 Tons

QUASI LEGAL LOS ANGELES COUNTY

OUTBUILDINGS = 400 Square feet maximum + 35 feet height maximum.

4

DECK w/ RAIL
quasi legal

BEDROOM

BATHROOM

KITCHEN

LIVING ROOM

BASEMENT
quasi legal

SPIRAL STAIRCASE
8ft. Top to Bottom

1 foot
8 feet
1 foot
8 feet
1 foot
8 feet
1 foot
8 feet

5 feet

STEEL I BEAMS

INSIDE & OUTSIDE WALLS
SMOOTH FINISH stucco over
STEEL MESH

GLASS BLOCK (TYPICAL runs at every
every side excep
glass plate

SLIDING GLASS PLATE

GROUND LE

CEMENT BLOCK

10 feet

10 feet

Chris Burden 19

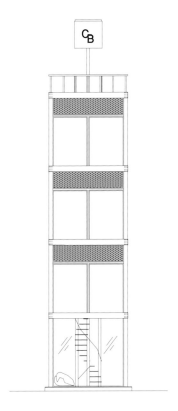

Standard Elevation

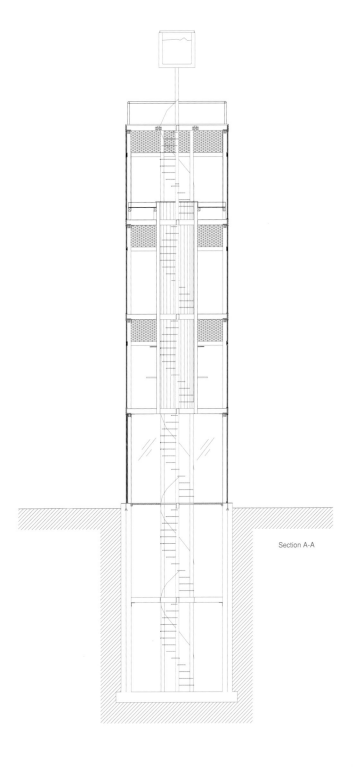

Section A-A

CANNOT BE
SEEN EXCEPT
FROM DIRECTLY
ABOVE!

MINI
SCRAPER

DEEP IN
THE LAND

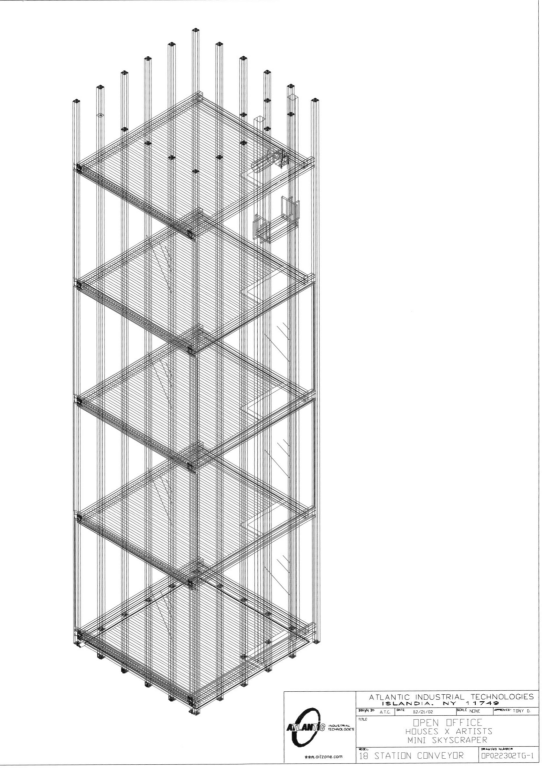

ATLANTIC INDUSTRIAL TECHNOLOGIES
ISLANDIA, NY 11749

| DRAWN BY A.T.G. | DATE 02/21/02 | SCALE NONE | APPROVED TONY G. |

TITLE:
OPEN OFFICE
HOUSES X ARTISTS
MINI SKYSCRAPER

MODEL
18 STATION CONVEYOR

DRAWING NUMBER
OP022302TG-1

ATLANTIC INDUSTRIAL TECHNOLOGIES

www.aitzone.com

NEIGHBOR'S HOUSE

MY HOU

MINI SCRAPER ON LITTLE MESA

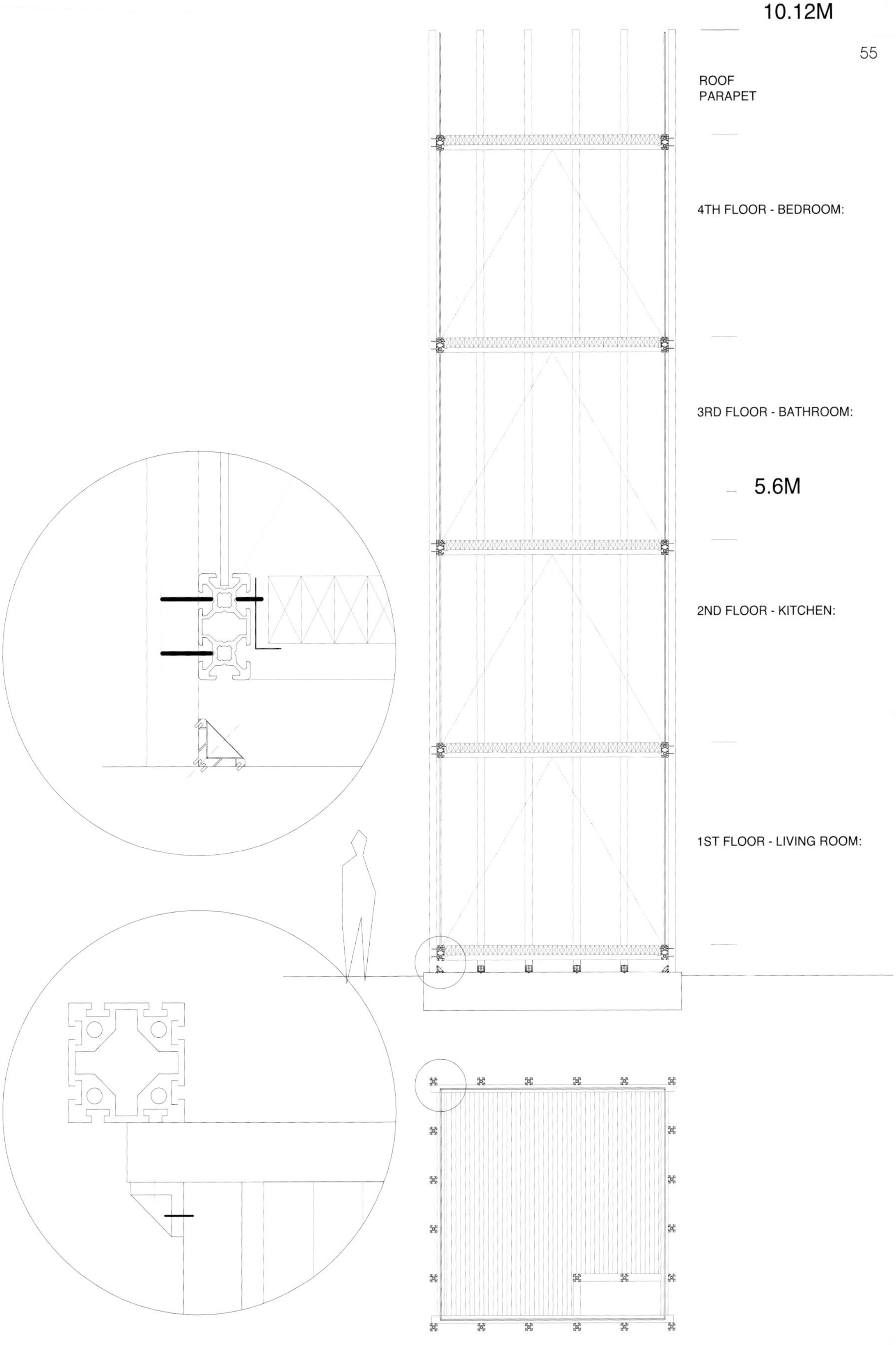

10.12M

ROOF
PARAPET

4TH FLOOR - BEDROOM:

3RD FLOOR - BATHROOM:

5.6M

2ND FLOOR - KITCHEN:

1ST FLOOR - LIVING ROOM:

JIM ISERMANN
YELLOW ROOF
MODULAR PANELS

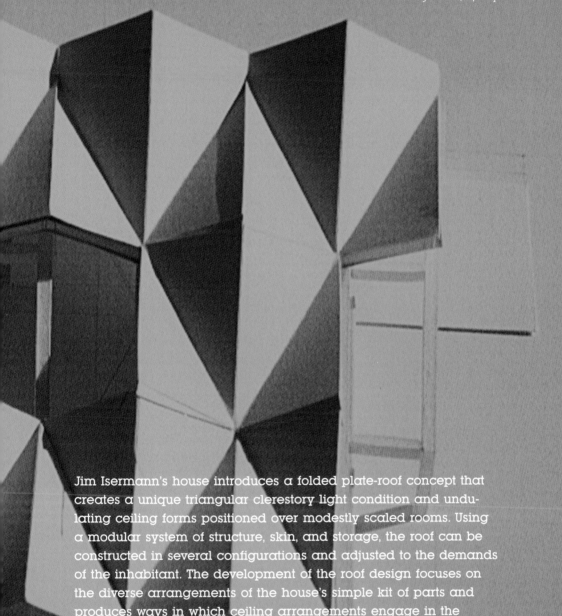

Jim Isermann's house introduces a folded plate-roof concept that
creates a unique triangular clerestory light condition and undulating ceiling forms positioned over modestly scaled rooms. Using
a modular system of structure, skin, and storage, the roof can be
constructed in several configurations and adjusted to the demands
of the inhabitant. The development of the roof design focuses on
the diverse arrangements of the house's simple kit of parts and
produces ways in which ceiling arrangements engage in the
creation of unusual architectural environments.

      Specific materials take on an important role in the flexi-
bility and freedom of the house; a steel structure allows for a free
plan, glazed brick is used as a wall and tile floor surface and
color treatment, and molded plastic resin roof panels provide
choice of clear or opaque shelter. The roof planes meet the house
walls and clerestory windows in multifaceted intersections that
become the site for structural and spatial invention.

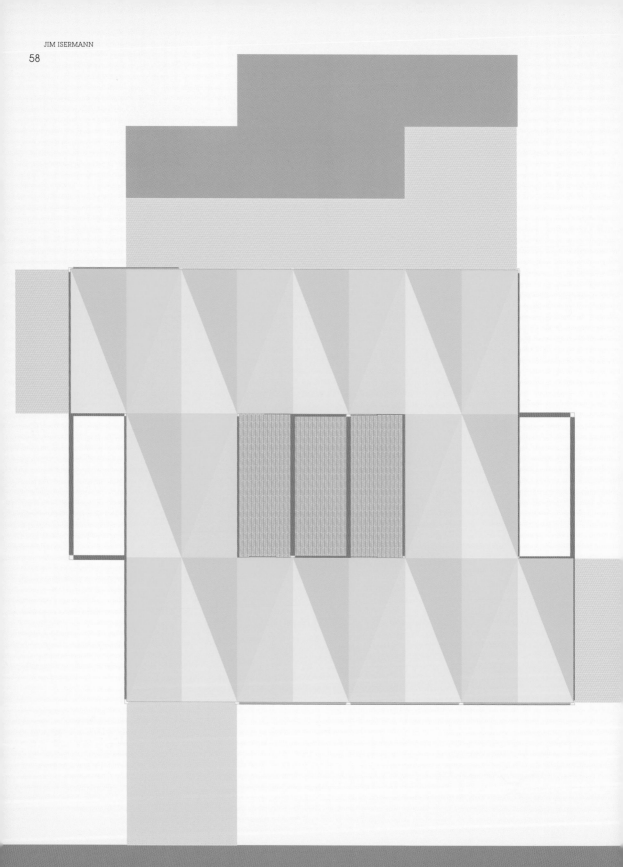

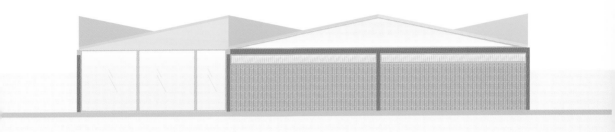

ELEVATION

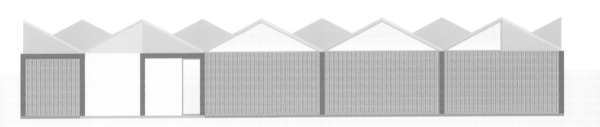

ELEVATION

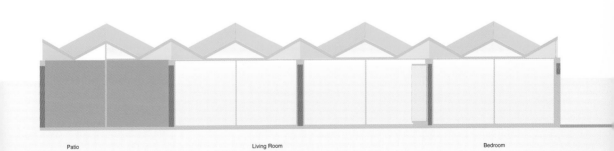

Patio   Living Room   Bedroom

SECTION THRU LIVING ROOM / BEDROOM

Living Room / Media Wall   Court   Studio

SECTION THRU COURTYARD

Garage   Studio   Bedroom   Patio

SECTION THRU GARAGE / STUDIO / BEDROOM

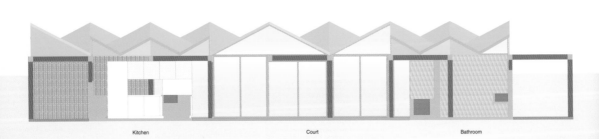

Kitchen   Court   Bathroom

SECTION THRU COURTYARD

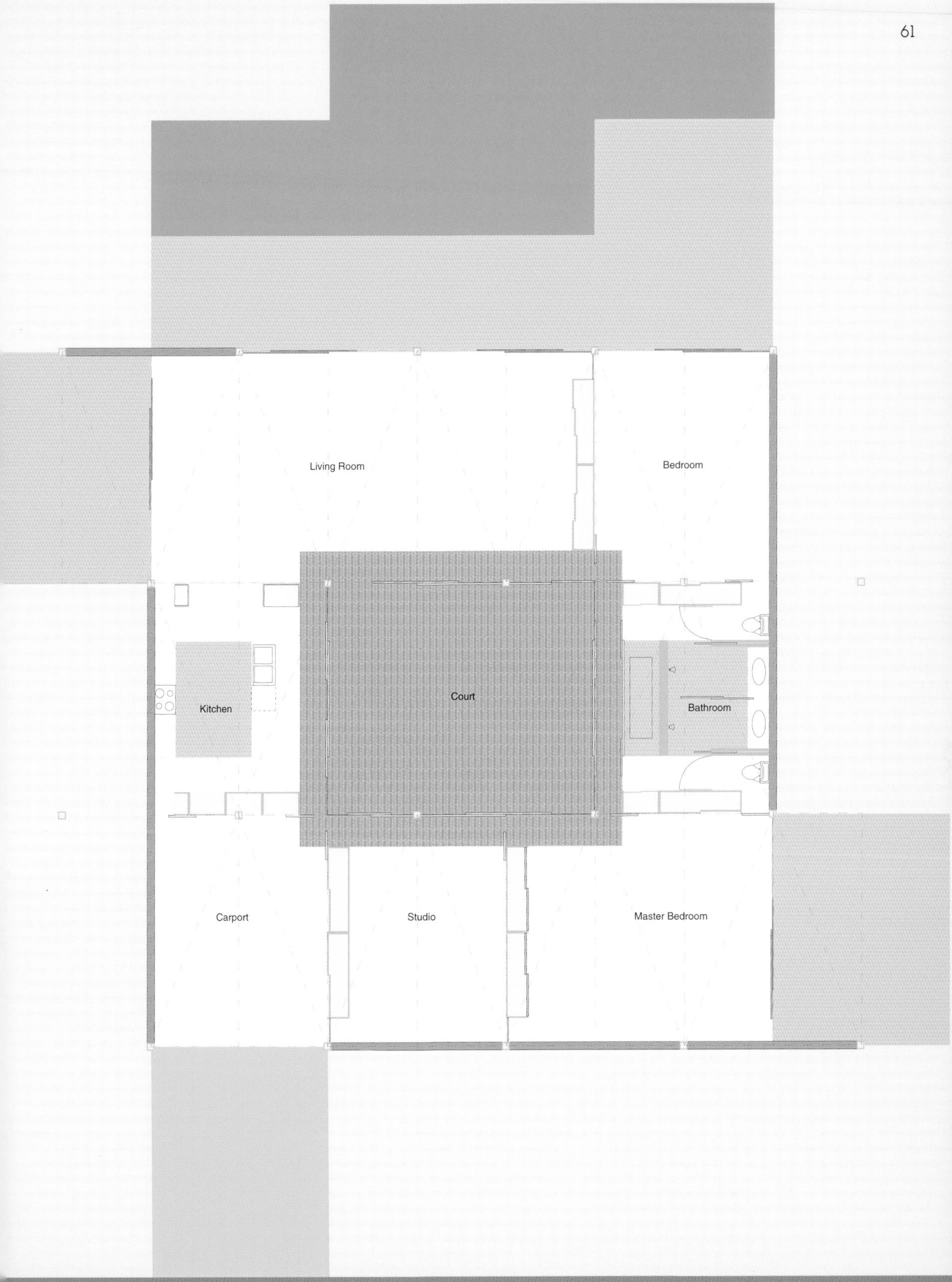

Living Room

Bedroom

Kitchen

Court

Bathroom

Carport

Studio

Master Bedroom

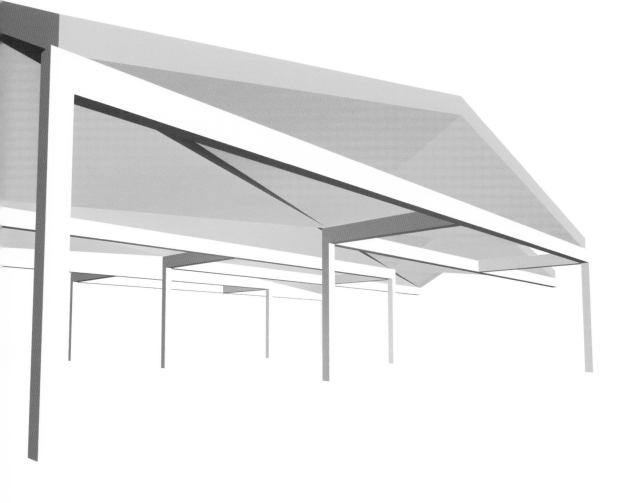

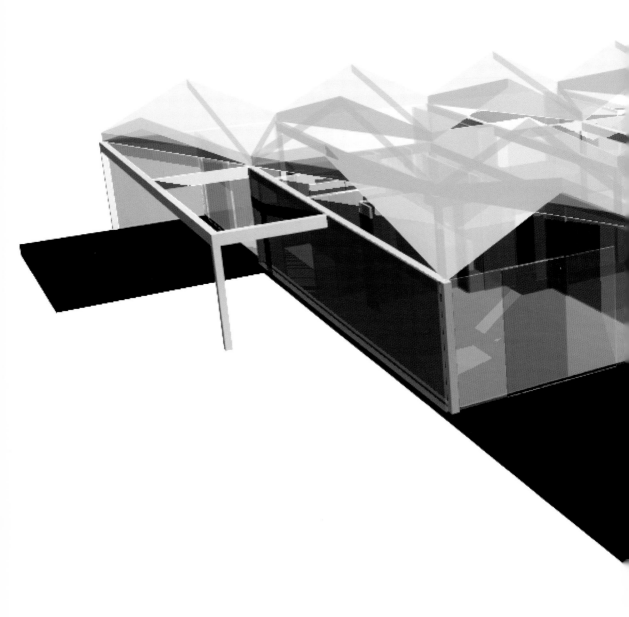

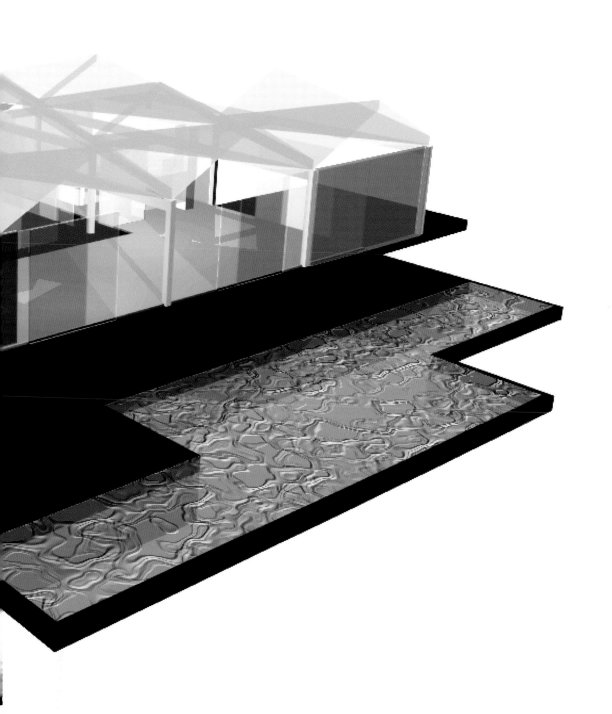

T. KELLY MASON: MODULES AND ARRANGEMENTS

T. Kelly Mason casts the house as an assemblage of ideas of prefabricated spaces—rooms that are as detachable and flexible as furniture. The structure draws from both existing domestic and industrial building systems and technologies as well as from invented furniture typologies. The spaces between rooms where walls usually occur create a public common space that invites the occupants to prescribe function. Thus the house functions as a landscape of familiar domestic spaces and unexpected open common spaces allowing the user to create a normal dwelling experience alongside a personal public zone of multifarious program.

The house is developed conceptually as a working machine designed, ultimately, to make its owner take responsibility for a series of aesthetic decisions. The house's component-like system seeks to eliminate the need for specialized construction knowledge through its simplicity and ease of installation; all parts are produced on an assembly line and pre-ordered from a catalogue. Parts would be delivered to the site on a flatbed truck and subjectively arranged to the owner's requirements and desires, a process similar to an architect's or a sculptor's activity of placing objects in space in relation to one another.

Combining established systems of mass production, prefabrication, and transportation with artistic decision making increases user flexibility, freedom, and activity in the building of a home. Given the subjective nature of the owners' arrangements of houses, industrial shell(s), and components, a community of this new type would reflect its local idiosyncratic qualities. The successful distribution of this building system is the realization of a large-scale sculpture, including factory, catalogue, and houses in one seamless, community created product.

KM00

KM Studio
7013 North Figueroa Street
Los Angeles
CA90042

KM is a subsidiary of K-MOO

Dear Investor:

Allow us to present you with the opportunity to invest in a housing system for the twenty-first century. This new product is perfectly situated to fulfill the needs of today's thinking consumer. It has been said that today's consumer doesn't want more choices, just better things. What today's housing consumer needs is a better choice. Our home design offers not only a better choice for the homebuyer, but a fantastic opportunity for an investor or investment group.

Our design:
· Can be built on any suitable piece of property.
· Production will be farmed out to existing manufacturing concerns, maximizing capital that has already been invested into the marketplace, and minimizing risk.
· Factory produced, insulating the investor from fluctuations in construction time and cost.
· Appeals to a mid level and above suburban home buyer or developer with a concern for aesthetics and environmental impact while maintaining an up-scale approach to quality and an extremely competitive price point.

· All that remains is the tooling, production, and retailing of the homes!

This is where you come in. We are seeking an initial investment of 15 million dollars. We feel that the chances for a high return on investment are excellent!

T. Kelly Mason
VP of Sales (Los Angeles)

The basics of the design consist of an outer building. What we call the structure and enclosure, is a simply constructed building of variable size. Into this structure and enclosure are inserted up to four basic interior modules. These modules provide the necessities of basic dwelling—kitchen, bedroom, bathroom, and den—and yet they provide much more than that! The modules themselves resolve the basic problems of shelter and privacy with user-friendly scale and flexibility.

The design invites the end-user to participate in the arrangement of the modules. The spaces in between the individual modules make up the remainder of the living space: entry halls, dining and living rooms, a home office, storage areas, etc. The placement of the modules and the positioning of their multifunctional exterior surfaces determine all these spaces. Some modules have shelving and closets integral to their exterior surfaces. Doors and windows can be interchanged to create new interior passageways or vistas. Part, but not all, of each unit can be placed outside of the enclosure.

Not only are the modules flexible in terms of their initial arrangement, but they are easily reconfigured as needs change. The system is engineered so that all but the most drastic changeover in design can be accomplished in one day's time.

Sales persons are provided with a standardized series of forms and calculations. This makes it a snap to determine parts lists and component possibilities within a given lot square footage.

2BDRM +2BA

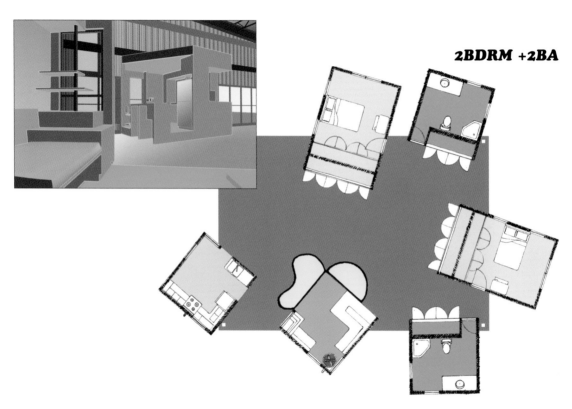

1BDRM +1BA

1BDRM +1BA

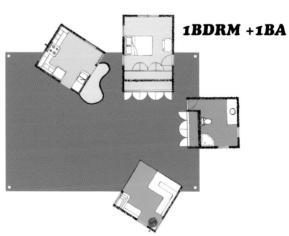

Today's housing industry has failed to address the shopping habits of the twenty-first century consumer.

Until now!

Choose options and accessories!

Arrange them to suit your lifestyle!

1 shell not enough? Use 2!

Start small and grow with your needs!

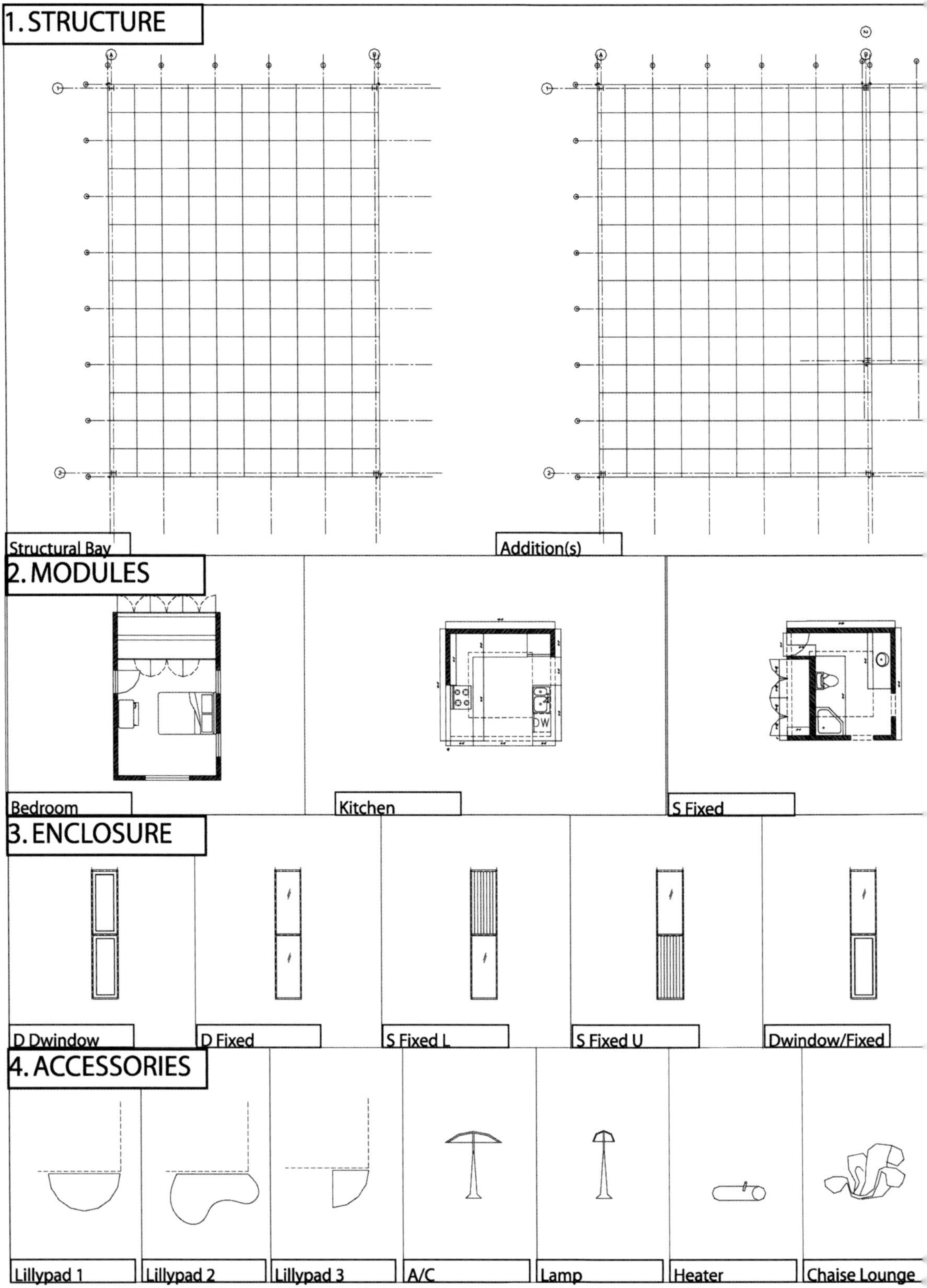

1. STRUCTURE

Structural Bay

Addition(s)

2. MODULES

Bedroom

Kitchen

S Fixed

3. ENCLOSURE

D Dwindow

D Fixed

S Fixed L

S Fixed U

Dwindow/Fixed

4. ACCESSORIES

Lillypad 1

Lillypad 2

Lillypad 3

A/C

Lamp

Heater

Chaise Lounge

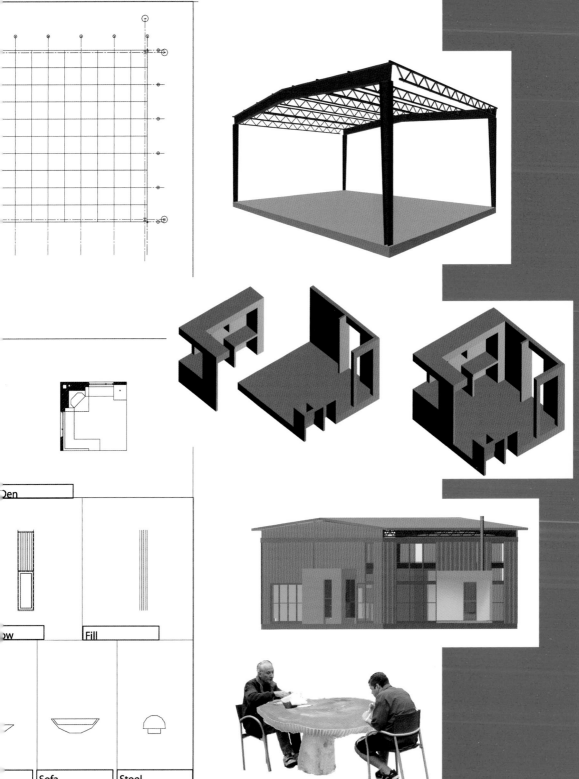

Den

ow

Fill

Sofa

Stool

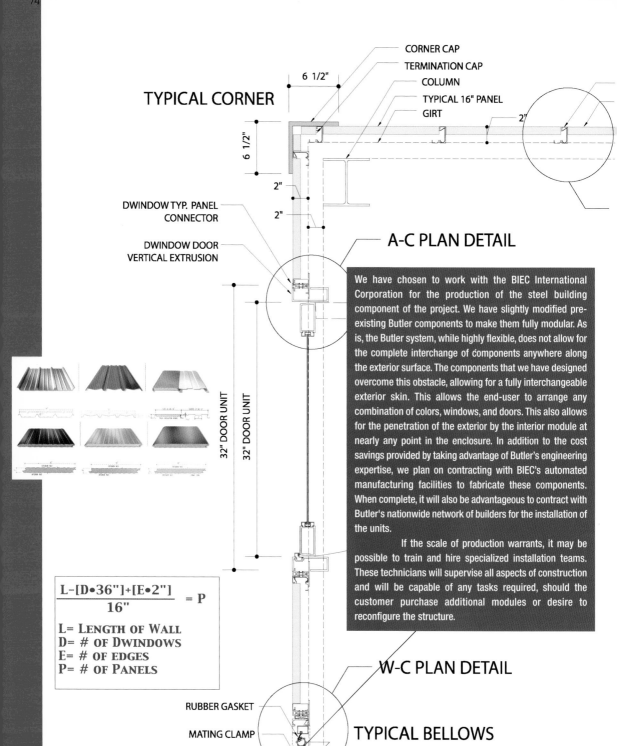

TYPICAL CORNER

CORNER CAP
TERMINATION CAP
COLUMN
TYPICAL 16" PANEL
GIRT

6 1/2"

6 1/2"

2"

2"

2"

DWINDOW TYP. PANEL CONNECTOR

DWINDOW DOOR VERTICAL EXTRUSION

A-C PLAN DETAIL

32" DOOR UNIT

32" DOOR UNIT

We have chosen to work with the BIEC International Corporation for the production of the steel building component of the project. We have slightly modified pre-existing Butler components to make them fully modular. As is, the Butler system, while highly flexible, does not allow for the complete interchange of components anywhere along the exterior surface. The components that we have designed overcome this obstacle, allowing for a fully interchangeable exterior skin. This allows the end-user to arrange any combination of colors, windows, and doors. This also allows for the penetration of the exterior by the interior module at nearly any point in the enclosure. In addition to the cost savings provided by taking advantage of Butler's engineering expertise, we plan on contracting with BIEC's automated manufacturing facilities to fabricate these components. When complete, it will also be advantageous to contract with Butler's nationwide network of builders for the installation of the units.

If the scale of production warrants, it may be possible to train and hire specialized installation teams. These technicians will supervise all aspects of construction and will be capable of any tasks required, should the customer purchase additional modules or desire to reconfigure the structure.

$$\frac{L-[D \cdot 36"]+[E \cdot 2"]}{16"} = P$$

L= LENGTH OF WALL
D= # OF DWINDOWS
E= # OF EDGES
P= # OF PANELS

W-C PLAN DETAIL

RUBBER GASKET

MATING CLAMP

TYPICAL BELLOWS

TYPICAL PLASTIC ROOM MODULE

3. ENCLOSURE

D Dwindow	D Fixed	S Fixed L	S Fixed U	Dwindow/Fixed	Dwindow	Fill

NEL JOINT

PANEL

PLAN DETAIL

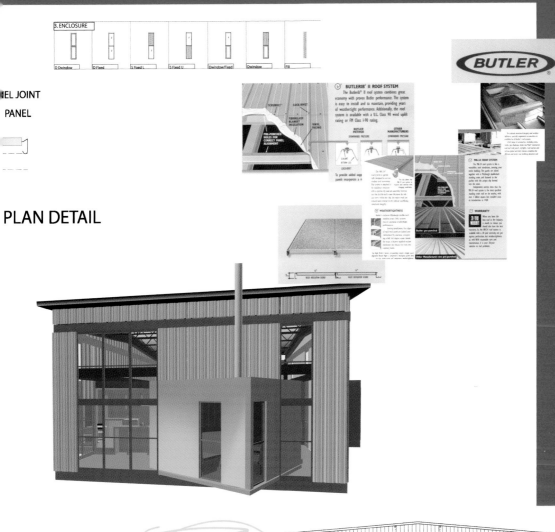

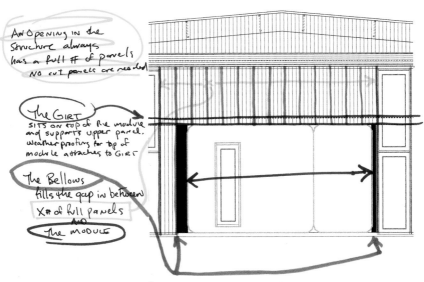

AN opening in the
Structure always
has a full # of panels
NO cut panels are needed

The GIRT
SITS on top of the module
and supports upper panel.
weatherproofing for top of
module attaches to GIRT

The Bellows
fills the gap in between
X# of full panels
AND
The MODULE

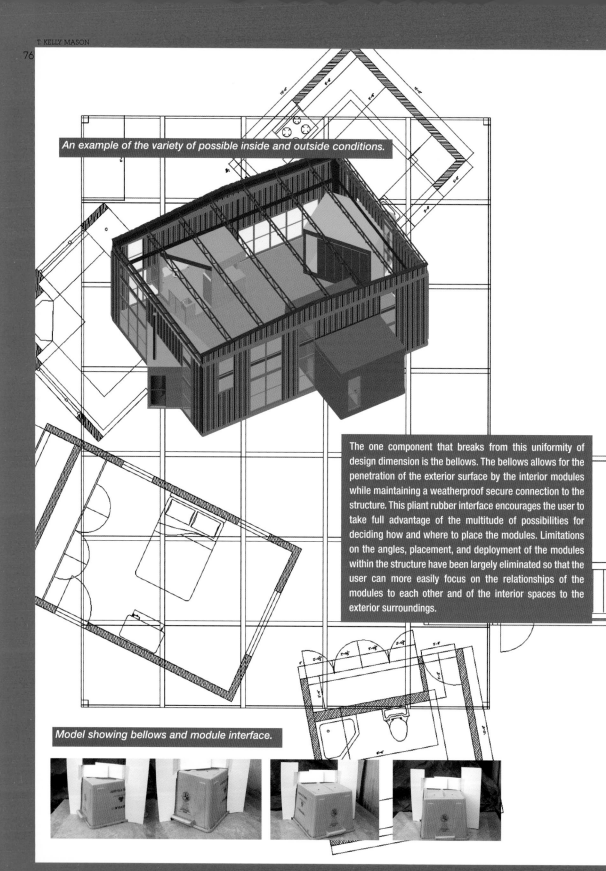

An example of the variety of possible inside and outside conditions.

The one component that breaks from this uniformity of design dimension is the bellows. The bellows allows for the penetration of the exterior surface by the interior modules while maintaining a weatherproof secure connection to the structure. This pliant rubber interface encourages the user to take full advantage of the multitude of possibilities for deciding how and where to place the modules. Limitations on the angles, placement, and deployment of the modules within the structure have been largely eliminated so that the user can more easily focus on the relationships of the modules to each other and of the interior spaces to the exterior surroundings.

Model showing bellows and module interface.

The modules will be fabricated using the rotational molding process. Rotomolding dramatically increases our ability to move beyond traditional design boundaries. Large-scale parts can be molded economically and produced in a variety of shapes and sizes, many of which would be impossible to produce by any other process. In Rotomolding, the plastic is placed into large steel molds, which are then heated and spun at a very high rate of speed. Though it has a high startup cost, the long life span of the molds (greater than 10,000 casts per mold) makes this process highly cost effective over the course of a production run. The savings in labor costs over traditionally built housing will far outweigh any additional costs of materials.

390° Slide Mold
Three piece mold with two cast insert.
(108" high x 82" diameter)

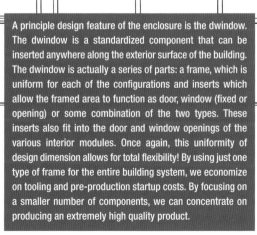

A principle design feature of the enclosure is the dwindow. The dwindow is a standardized component that can be inserted anywhere along the exterior surface of the building. The dwindow is actually a series of parts: a frame, which is uniform for each of the configurations and inserts which allow the framed area to function as door, window (fixed or opening) or some combination of the two types. These inserts also fit into the door and window openings of the various interior modules. Once again, this uniformity of design dimension allows for total flexibility! By using just one type of frame for the entire building system, we economize on tooling and pre-production startup costs. By focusing on a smaller number of components, we can concentrate on producing an extremely high quality product.

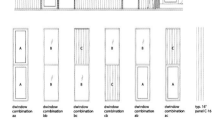

dwindow combination aa

dwindow combination bb

dwindow combination bc

dwindow combination cb

dwindow combination ab

dwindow combination ac

typ. 16" panel C-16

Bedroom

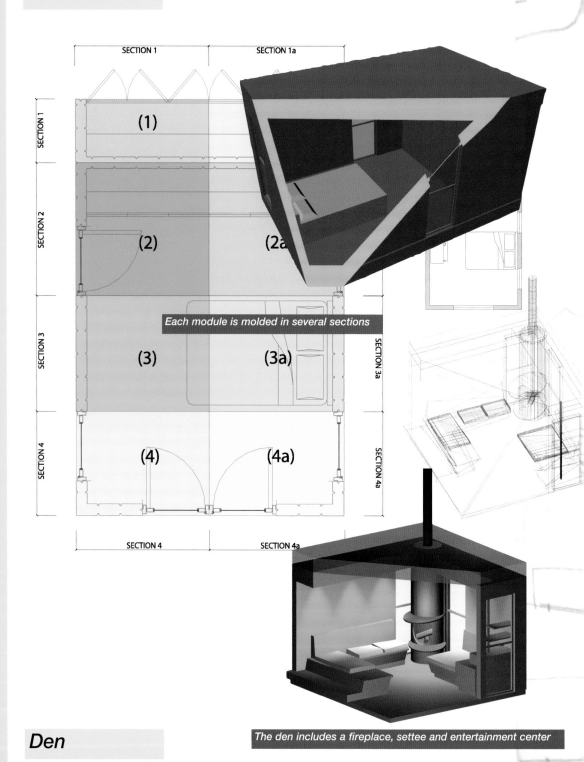

SECTION 1   SECTION 1a

SECTION 1

(1)

SECTION 2

(2)   (2a)

Each module is molded in several sections

SECTION 3

(3)   (3a)

SECTION 3a

SECTION 4

(4)   (4a)

SECTION 4a

SECTION 4   SECTION 4a

The den includes a fireplace, settee and entertainment center

Den

Kitchen

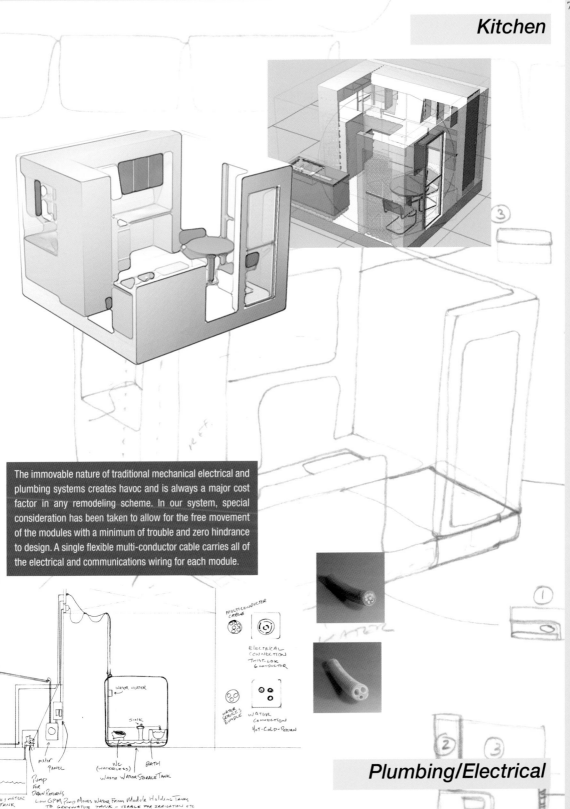

The immovable nature of traditional mechanical electrical and plumbing systems creates havoc and is always a major cost factor in any remodeling scheme. In our system, special consideration has been taken to allow for the free movement of the modules with a minimum of trouble and zero hindrance to design. A single flexible multi-conductor cable carries all of the electrical and communications wiring for each module.

MULTI CONDUCTOR CABLE

ELECTRICAL CONNECTION TWIST-LOK 6 CONDUCTOR

WATER SERVICE BUNDLE

WATER CONNECTION HOT-COLD-RETURN

WATER HEATER

SINK

METER PANEL

WC (WATERLESS) WASTE WATER STORAGE TANK

BATH

GREYWATER TANK

PUMP FOR DRAIN RETURNS

LOW GPM PUMP MOVES WATER FROM MODULE HOLDING TANKS TO GREYWATER TANK - USABLE FOR IRRIGATION ETC

Plumbing/Electrical

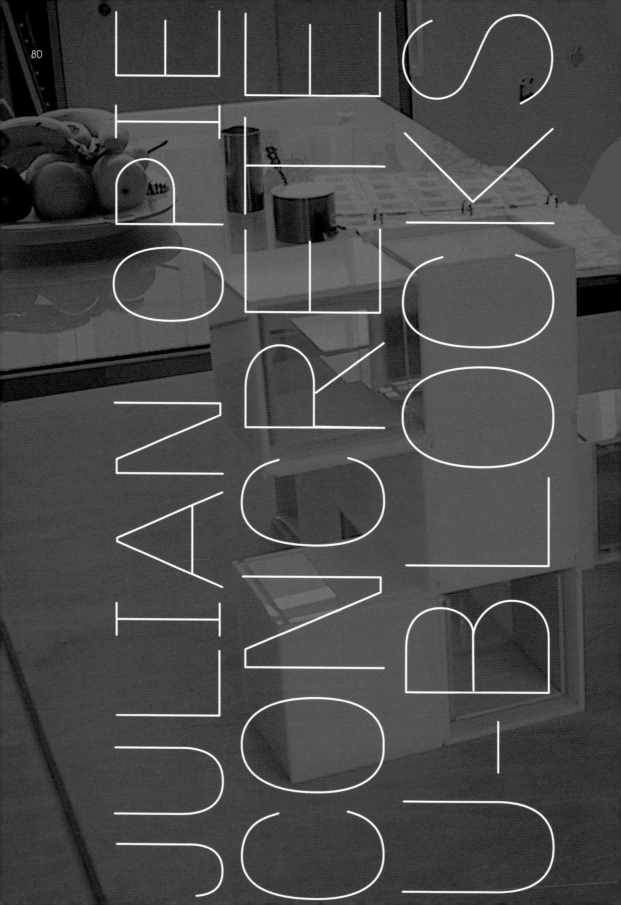

JULIAN OPIE CONCRETE U-BLOCKS

Julian Opie's house accepts the site of non-site as a pre-condition for the modern house and proposes a prefabricated building typology that can be configured on a case-by-case basis. The scheme places emphasis on the elegance imposed by the limits such a system requires while paradoxically capitalizing on the unusual meta-forms that will emerge from the struggle to formalize the dweller's personal domestic appetites.

The structure is comprised of a system of nested units, each system providing a greater degree of flexibility than the one encasing it. Units can be combined in a number of arrangements, determined by the owner's needs or desires or in response to specific site conditions. The exterior unit is a basic structure/enclosure (3m x 3m) prefabricated as a concrete "U".

The second sub-system is a glass enclosure of windows and skylights for environmental control. The third element is an interior wood-paneling system as well as a complex built-in furniture system providing interior finishes, storage, and cabinetry modules, service cavities and plenums, as well as pass-through partitions and privacy sub-sections. The last sub-section is a continuous curtain system for fluid day-to-day spatial definition, privacy, and comfort.

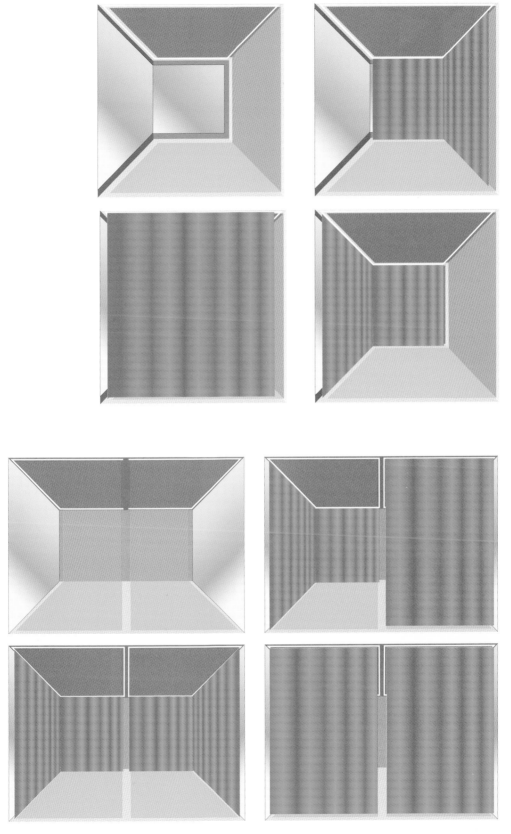

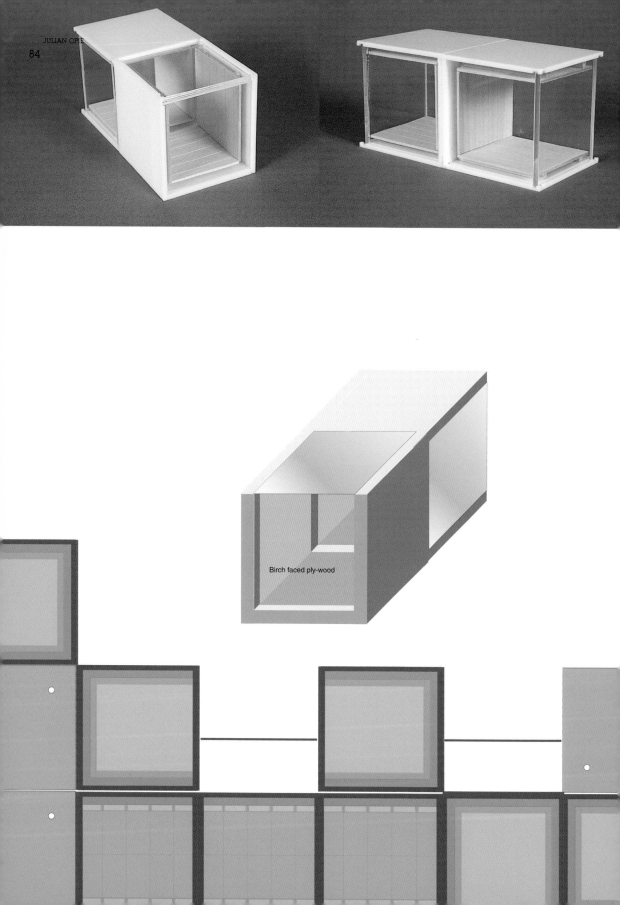

Birch faced ply-wood

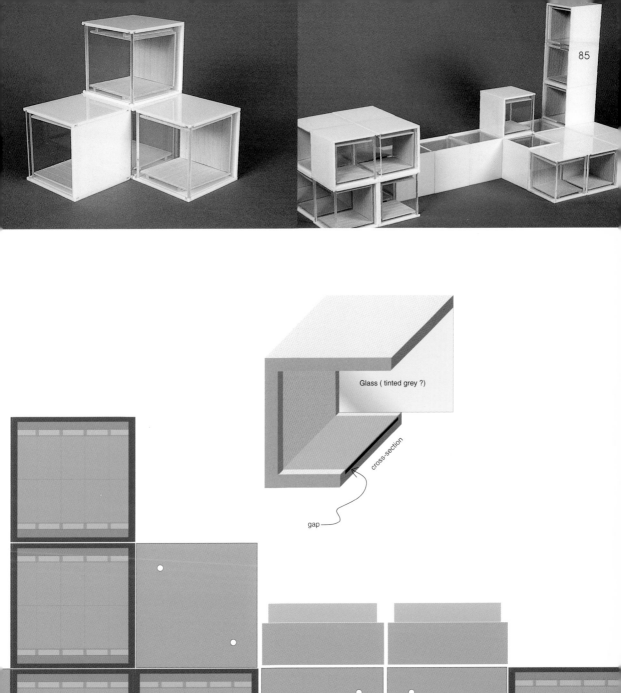

85

Glass (tinted grey ?)

cross-section

gap

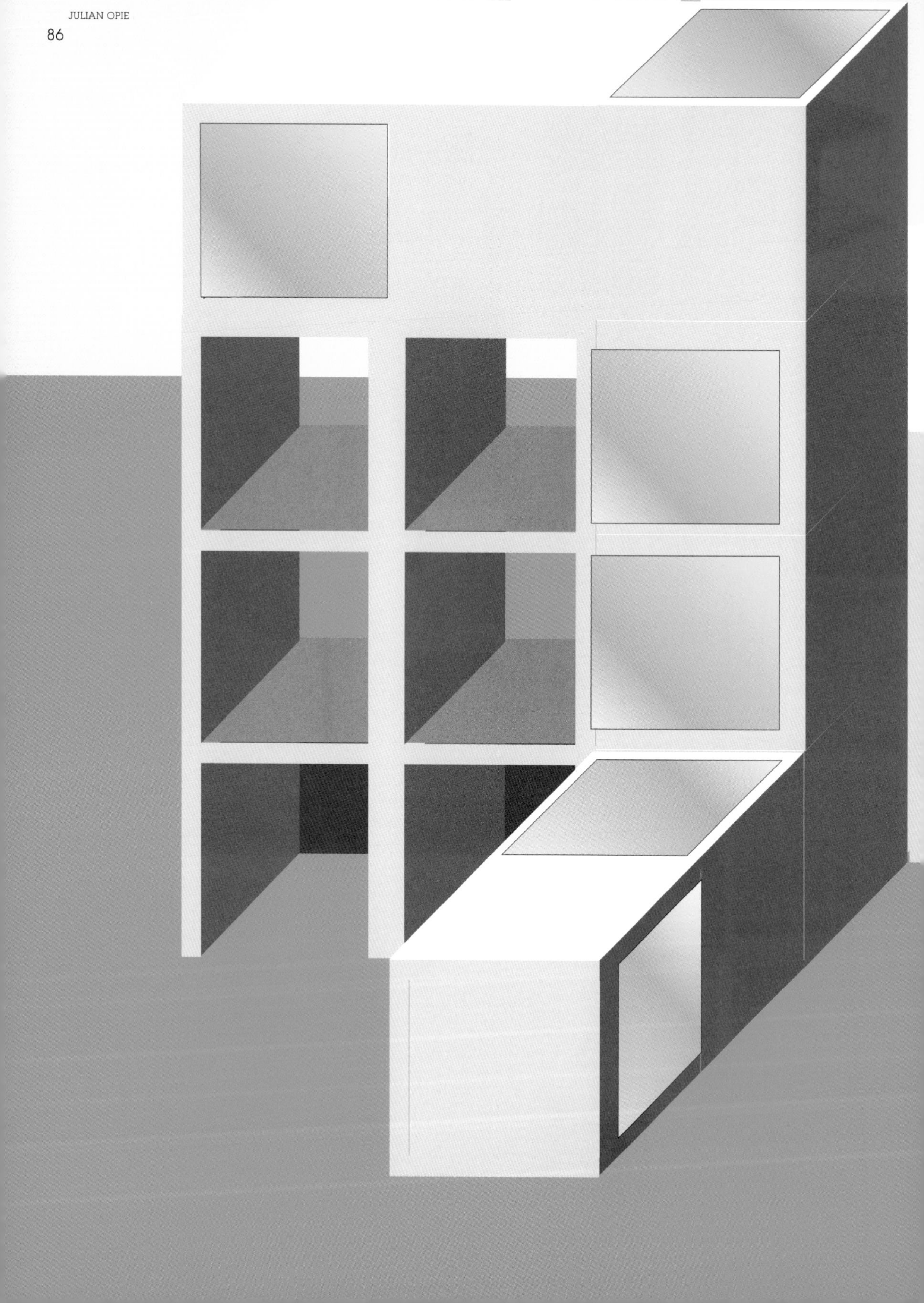

RENÉE PETROPOULOS

EXIT

CONNOTATION

GAS STATION

MINIMART CLIPS

Renée Petropoulos posits a dwelling structure formed exclusively
from cultural success stories. Rather than relying on given abstract
building conventions such as nominal timber and the like, or rational
overlays such as the uncontested Cartesian grid, Petropoulos seeks to
find the ways in which the formal elements of popular conventions
(markets, airports, French gardens, Islamic mosques) can be over-
lapped, superimposed, and re-used at the domestic scale, while
retaining their imbedded cues for successful inhabitation. Like the
Piazza Navona in Rome, formed directly out of the foundation ruins of
the ancient Circus Maximus, the formal make-up of an abandoned
use can translate directly into a shifted set of demands, and thereby
enrich the new use to a greater level than "pure design" could on its
own. Petropoulos's house uses the gas station mini-market as a
model. The investigation distills a time-tested set of architectural
devices used for mediating between people in various scales and
balances of social exchange. Her house design is a case study into
the social traits embedded in a given vernacular; the rules uncover
a set of guidelines for her multiple future house designs, easily
mapped into various dwelling programs such as multiple family
occupations or time-share vacation properties.

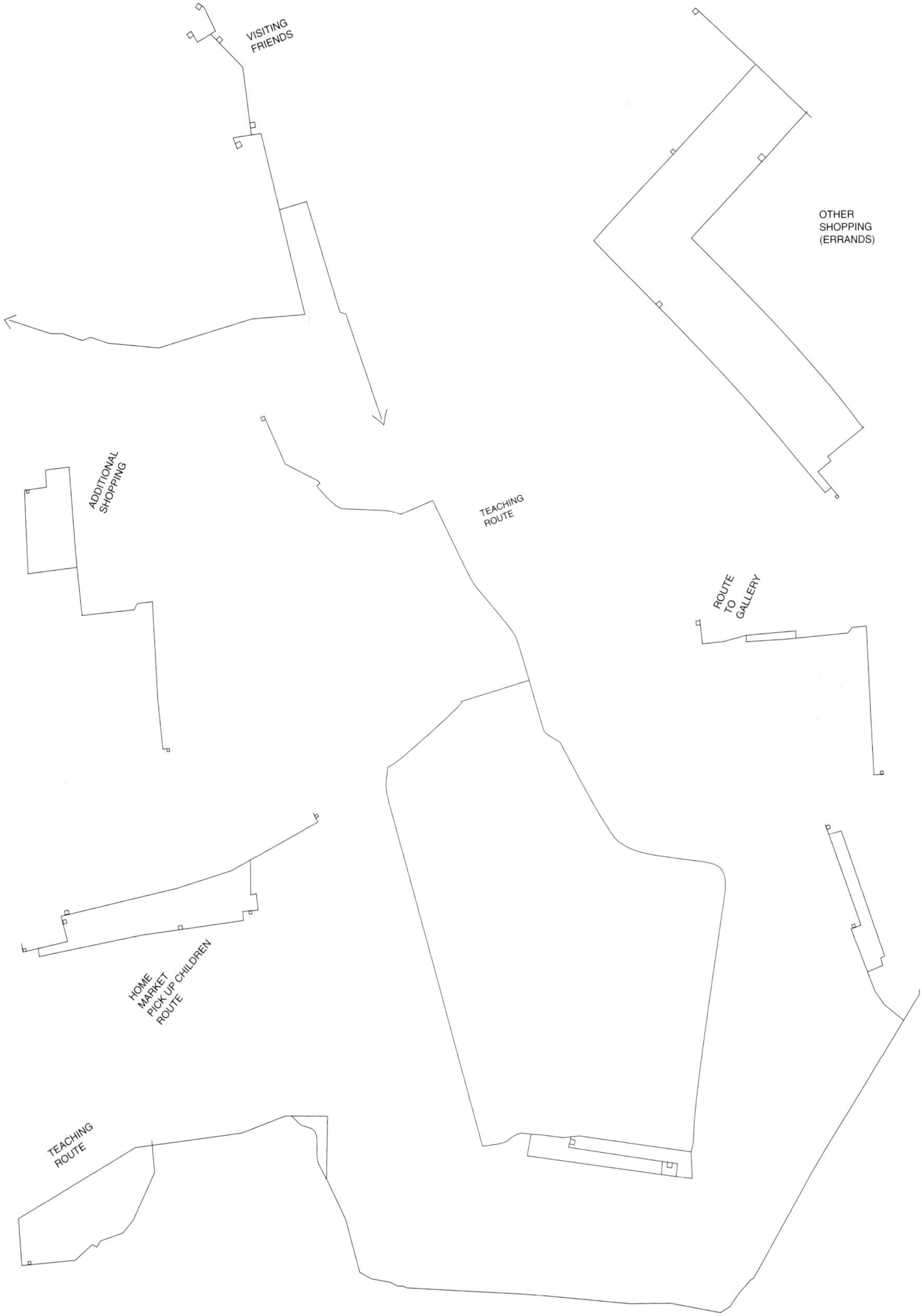

VISITING
FRIENDS

OTHER
SHOPPING
(ERRANDS)

ADDITIONAL
SHOPPING

TEACHING
ROUTE

ROUTE
TO
GALLERY

HOME
MARKET
PICK UP CHILDREN
ROUTE

TEACHING
ROUTE

notes from the minimart

thank you these are good there are some right here do you want to sure thank you all right ladies go sit down at the table how about that on the right side what are you doing you go and eat gimmie that *your going to be a star you're going be a star just about enough just about enough still in love with you cry'in can't take anymore you won't give me what I deserve got to get away from you* buh bye tell her I'm ready yeah I'm almost done let me go see ali how are you five minutes no okay bye okay thanks a lot credit card cash thank you yeah we can number four I don't know not so much really good prices keep working for what this is it this is wrong man okay credit card cash thank you *know my name so in love with I see the fair moon arisin'in what's go'in on ain't no woman like the one I got (3 times) oh come all ye faithful joyful and triumphant Have yourself a merry little christ-mas now... and a shinning star upon the highest bough* is that you *everyday the sun comes up around you hey you ain't no woman like the one I love music in my all right then ain't no woman like the one I got so together like a hand in glove* ohhhlaughter I'm going to go see oh my god three there is some-thing about tanks number 15 number 15 number 16 number 18 number 18 number 19 number 21 that's part of it go flirt go on I want to be like that I don't know are people more into their partners than people who are married a soda I need a haircut margie had a nervous breakdown now she's on the mend rebound from the she's very beautiful argentinian never had a wild phase oh my boring life maybe its just me and my discontent with everything probably not that bad a little bit of thrill got to watch out do do do dum do do do do do... you can sit here the whole ensemble his brother go flirt I want to be like that oh my god there are three of them they are so boring how old are you fantastic I am 79 awesome whose brother does-n't like you of course what a mess what did you say I love this those are great I think we should go for never partied in college hi weeks later da da da ninety-nine hi hello I couldn't get my card to work in the machine 115 atm right fill up yeah I use it here all the time change on one ah thanks where's that for 2.69 we're all here for change today get in line buddy you shouldn't open your mouth of course I'm 1.49 thank you change on five have a good one ahhh should I get a bag a napkin hurry up 4.16 okay nine did you push the yellow button no push the yellow button 3.14 a half eaten hot dog 50 cents right I got it it was half eaten.

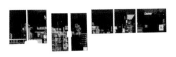

notes from the conversation

Preliminary development proposed a house as a composite of sites—public spaces—rooted in the historical, but conscious and inclusive of the contemporary—mosques, Japanese tearooms, airline terminals, nineteenth-century gardens, Piazza del Popolo, fast food restaurants… As the development of the design progressed, concerns regarding the sprawling nature of the project, both conceptually and literally, exposed themselves. It became clear that a single model that included the functions of the other models could be used, the model is the contemporary gas station minimart (GSMM) or "stop-n-go". The GSMM has an incredible function to provide food, rest and relief to the mobile society; it accommodates the car, provides social interaction, reflects the beliefs of consumerism, and thrives by its "undesigned" characteristic—its central yet marginal status in the world of buildings. Who designs the gas station minimart? Who takes credit for its arrangement?

The house design is based in the researching of the GSMM model. The resultant house reflects and also departs from this origin, as we propose a very different function. The experience of the house echoes the GSMM interactive social space and fleeting service oriented quality, creating a space of domestic transcience.

RENÉE: The GSMMs use is determined by its appropriated function as a domestic dwelling. There's no real difference in the actual plan or shape of the space in its assertion for different programs. It's not designed to be a kitchen or to be a bedroom or be a living room. It always has the same components. You just put different furniture in it—you use it differently. But there's no inherent designing that takes place to make it something else.

ALAN: Are there scale shifts at all?

RENÉE: No. The bedroom would be the same size as another room.

ALAN: Do you think people could treat it more like a loft space?

RENÉE: All the necessities of domesticity would be available—which "room" is what designation would be determined by the occupant.

LINDA: Well, the unit might be made up of different minimarts. It could become quite complex as an object, even if those pieces that are attached onto it are stripped down.

RENÉE: It is necessary to understand that there is a model that the house is based upon, but that it is not an exact replication of the model. It is the form and its characteristics that get carried over. Its use in one context and its use in another context is something quite different.

RENÉE: The exhibition will use a variety of media to show the research of the GSMM, from film and video, to sound, to architectural plans and models. A combination of things will be seen in the exhibition film; like the garbage area or the bathroom or these funny hallways forming a kind of break in logic. If you see the graphic depictions and then you see it stripped away as a abstraction, then new connections will be made by the viewer as it comes together.

RENÉE: I was thinking of the film having really no sound track; but that sound could be another component in the exhibition. You could put on a headset or listen to it. Rather than attaching them to each other you could watch the images. One aspect is not prioritized over another.

ALAN: And they're not synched.

RENÉE: Yes. And you could also have the sound on while you're looking at the drawings.

LINDA: All the different media we use will be looking at the same thing but not necessarily in synchrony. In the end producing a kind of reading that in itself is not definitive. Ultimately the user would come in and arrange this information and subsequently the house's rooms however they perceive them and need them to be.

RENÉE: Yes. And that's the way the house is particularized to whoever the occupant is. Because they determine how the room is used rather than the architect or the designer determining that this is what this room is for. However at the moment we are the occupant for the sake of the current design.

ALAN: The idea is that the house is not designed, because it already exists. The more that you can take and re-adapt…

RENÉE: …the better. And that comes from really looking at the GSMM. I think that we all have experience with them. But until you look at the GSMM with a different mindset, it's not going to totally gel. Such as the way that counter is situated, does it sit by the front door? Or does it actually sit back in the space? is it floating? It's positioned to see the entire room.

RENÉE: There are types of things, like facades, interiors, layouts.

ALAN: Furniture.

RENÉE: Yes. The information could be organized as an archive, or indexical ordering. One page is just facade details, one windows, one doors, one signage. One page could be just the way the layout is.

LINDA: It could be a dictionary.

RENÉE: Yes, in a sense. A lexicon of these types of things.

RENÉE: And then there would be the CD part, so you can listen to what goes on in the GSMM, creating another layer. Then there is the process part where the drawings develop; looking at it like city map layouts and looking at how people converge or move around.

ALAN: But the drawings aren't going to be produced for the catalogue.

RENÉE: Actually it is this research that will ultimately produce the drawings.

LINDA: I think that's interesting in terms of an idea of an experiment. If we encapsulate the GSMM into a lexicon of images and memories of our observations prior to the drawing production; then we would be using it as a lexicon literally.

ALAN: The way that I'm seeing the catalogue, it's about recording the tropes of the different components of the GSMM. And then in the exhibition you have the catalogue in your hand. You see the tropes in color diagrams describing how they can go together in various ways. You hear the sound piece. You see the video investigation. And you have to reference the catalogue to understand the exhibition.

LINDA: This is a planning strategy, following a research project into typologies; where theaters were looked at, tatami mats etc… different structures were looked at, ultimately we settled on this particular planning typology.

RENÉE: Religious building. The fast-food mart… These structures were examined for their significance and their form — but they were too embedded in the historical model. And then it was edited down to the minimart, as being the typical, as a structure both literally and symbolically that could contain all of the "values" found in the assembly of models used previously.

LINDA: In other words, there's no idiosyncratic new thing that we're seeking to super-impose on top of the minimart. We're going to only use existing material that minimarts already use.

ALAN: As an example, we know that the minimart has a big glass section of wall. Can you replace the glass wall on just the bedroom unit? Because the idea is that it's a window. But if you don't actually need the glass, maybe you can just use a device that's a divider.

RENÉE: The Schindler House is the inversion of what I'm doing. It was conceived as a two-family house, a domestic space. And now it's functioning as a kind of open public forum. In a way that's why I want to do something to it; to have that kind of experience heightened. You could get to know that thinking about the work.

LINDA: And the GSMM has a social space that we are discovering. Such as that the skaters hang out over here by the back. And if this is a bedroom that space becomes the porch, because of its latent porch-like attraction to skaters.

RENÉE: Yes. And in one instance, it really is where trash cans go. The form is in place but its intended function differs by its use.

LINDA: Its function is the emotional or psychological mapped onto the practical. Properties could carry over, but functions could change.

RENÉE: The social political and geographical are also enormous influences on the form and the function. If it is indexed through the minimart as we're discussing; then my supposition is that the variations will be there. If you look at X number, you'll have X number of ways to approach it. You can change the material of it, but you understand the type through the lexicon.

ALAN: So it's really a point of reference of looking at other things in the world.

LINDA: It's a planning device.

RENÉE: It's a planning device, yes.

RENÉE: The plan that we first developed expanded physically and conceptually — it was becoming too expansive and too pastiche like. The GSMM is a public space of a certain type, that can be used freely. And you only need one of them. It's not necessary to represent every type any more, because one will do many things.

LINDA: This is a multi-functional, generic place.

RENÉE: Everything that we want exists in the minimart already. In the types that are already available, we've already seen stone and we've already seen open cinderblock, and we've already seen glass like this. So we don't need to go anywhere else but here.
The role of taste is not yet determined. I'm not sure if it makes any difference. We will make selections. The selections could be based on function, or reference, or the "readymade" (GSMM) and on us, and then the occupant would determine many particularities.

RENÉE: As we develop it, it's not going to really feel like a minimart any more. It will lose many of the characteristics. Because it won't have bags of chips and rows of the same kind of soda… it won't be inhabited in the same way.

LINDA: The refrigerators might become bookshelves, for example. They're shelves, they store things.

RENÉE: Yes, but they won't have to look like a refrigerator. There would just be a place where there would be shelving. It will lose the use of the minimart, because that's not useful to a home.

ALAN: Yes, but I know part of what you're interested in is the fact that you bump into these things and you're like: "Why is this here? I don't need a window between my living room and kitchen." The planning devices are fixed. And these are the things you bump into. But they've transformed and try to be more commodious.

RENÉE: Exactly. We might leave some of the structural devices if for example there are some poles holding up the roof… Every space that initially has these roof poles will require that the program reckon with that as a component. Or for example the location of the door; even though it would really be nicer to move the door, we would leave it in it original place. And then you have to work with how that functions. So there are certain things that remain fixed.

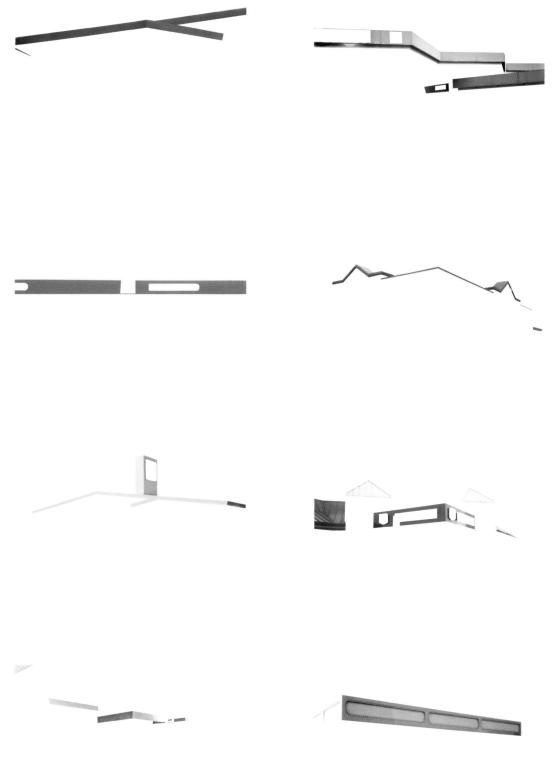

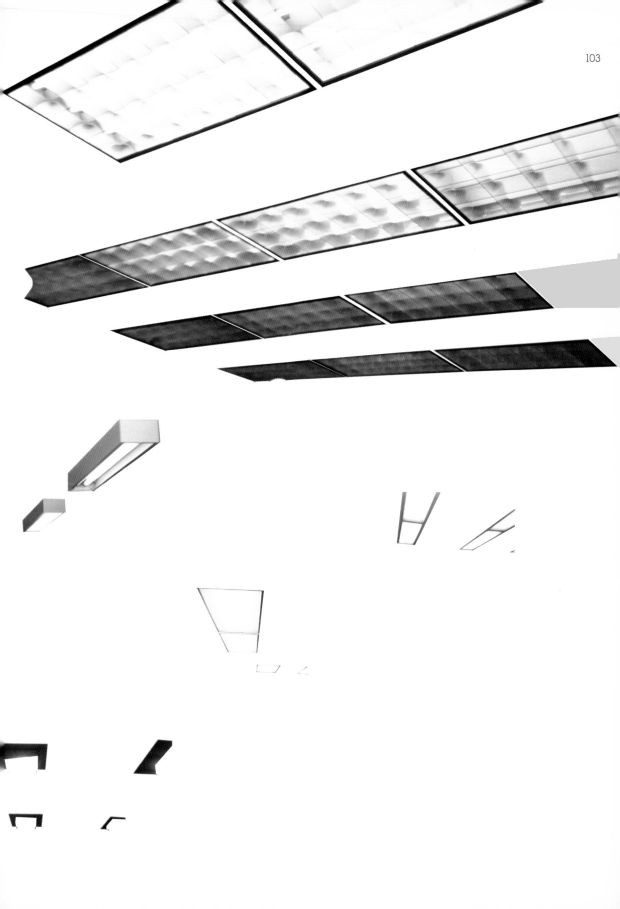

DAVID REED
PROCESS MODEL
INTERACTIVE INSTALLATION

104 *Charles-Louise Clérisseau, design for the "Ruin Room" at Stanta Trinita del Monte, Rome (1766)* 105
106 *Model, view of bedroom interior* | 107 *3-d rendering of spiral staircase for house proposal; model, exterior view with billboard-size image*
108 *Robert Smithson, Hotel Palenque (1969); Kings Road House, construction; Kings Road House, sleeping basket*
109 *Robert Smithson, Hotel Palenque (1969)* | 110 *Model, aerial view of exterior* | 112 *Charles-Louise Clérisseau, design for the "Ruin Room" at*
Stanta Trinita del Monte, Rome (1766); model, view from skylight | 113 *Model, view of bedroom interior*
114 *Kings Road House, construction; Kings Road House, construction* | 115 *Tilt-slab diagram* | 116 *Model, view of art loading vault*

For David Reed art is too frequently viewed in a conscious, analytical state of mind. Reed takes on a potential program for a collector's house and proposes instead a bedroom/gallery pavilion that aims to address this concern by positing a space for viewing art conducive to reverie rather than analysis—the private realm of the bedroom. Reed contends that this is the optimal modern space for a fluid and heightened state of awareness. The program resists the "white cube" tendency toward so-called "neutral" gallery space in favor of a complex and emotional spatial indeterminacy. Further, the idea of the house as an ideal architectural construct is also too analytic and restrictive; a built house can only be perfect in a structural sense the moment after its construction, before the building begins to deteriorate through user and environmental effects. Reed's proposal is therefore a space in flux, between a "construction site" and a "ruin."

Like the design concept, the proposed inhabitation allows for continual change and alteration. The house is comprised of a series of walls and partial enclosures that are assembled on the site in a seemingly haphazard way, but in actuality are ordered to a different set of needs and rules akin to a construction/ruin site; based on the needs of the collection the enclosure is flexible to accommodate changes in collecting interests. Given the nature of the partially closed and ever changing structure the house exists in an indoor and outdoor state of entropy, with specific elements of moving furniture and building material able to shift the locations and conditions of the program.

The bedroom is defined by the presence of two beds that slide freely on moving tracks from a shared communal space, which forms the main gallery, to discreet spaces that also serve as the public zones of the private dwelling—entrance and garden. Water elements for bathing, recreation, and site-enhancing occur throughout the house and site. The collection is stored in a large underground vault, conceived as a series of rooms organized strategically below the dry zones of the house connected to two openings to the above. One opening serves as a hydraulic lift to exhume and deposit works and the other serves as a light well under the beds in the communal gallery above, under which a scale model of the house with scale versions of the collection is installed for the planning of future building and curatorial installations.

Collecting is a way of thinking about alternative futures, a way to try to move the future in a desired direction. This bedroom/pavilion is designed to give an art collector a storage and viewing facility that fosters the concentration and openness required for this kind of thinking. My modest collection, with additional works by the same artists, serves as an example for the pavilion's use.

In the Disney version of *20,000 Leagues Under the Sea*, Captain Nemo's collection of paintings looks wonderful in the living area of the Nautilus, a futuristic submarine of his own design. In ornate frames, the landscape paintings don't fit into the alternate technological future postulated by the submarine, but contrary to expectations, this disjunction of the paintings from their surroundings serves to accentuate content rather than diminish it.

Paintings by Pam Fraser, Monique Prieto, Laura Owens

R. M. Schindler's house on Kings Road, which a friend calls "the spiritual center of Los Angeles," is a site similar to Nemo's Nautilus, in that it too proposes an idealistic future that was lost. In this case, the myth of unrealization takes the form of a failure of communal living, a failure that results in the division of the house. An emblem of this unrealized future is the paint that Pauline Schindler used to cover the concrete walls in her part of the house.

"It's not often that you see buildings being both ripped down and built up at the same time," Robert Smithson comments in his talk "Hotel Palenque." This describes the kind of space a collector needs, a bedroom/pavilion that is intimate, but also open and variable. Works can be tested in different situations—two moveable double beds in a space that is both under construction and in ruins.

Paintings by Ingrid Calame, Pam Fraser

Paintings by Monique Prieto, Laura Owens

Similarly, works can be seen in many different lighting situations:
under modulated sunlight falling through a skylight; in side-raking
daylight at sunset; under cool florescent and warm incandescent
electric lights; bathed in colored reflections from the garden or
from a flickering screen; in shadows cast by bonfires. *Paintings by Laura Owens, Pam Fraser*

Below ground, beneath the pavilion, is a large storage area for works of art, a library, and a scale model for planning the movements of works in the collection. When chosen to be lived with, a work is raised up on a hydraulic platform to be placed in the pavilion.

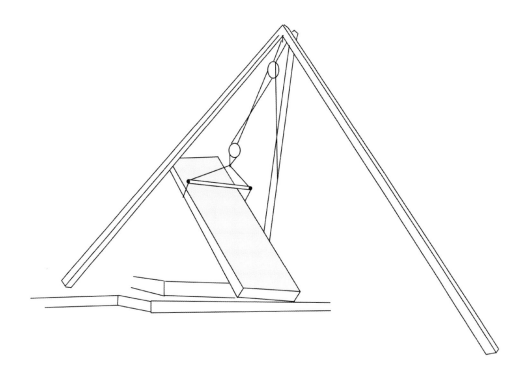

The pavilion could be used as a guest bedroom as well as a private viewing room.
This project is dedicated to Nicholas Wilder.

Paintings by Pam Fraser, Monique Prieto, Laura Owens

JESSICA STOCKHOLDER
PINK CONCRETE
TIMBER MODEL

Jessica Stockholder's house employs the typical, small house convention of a single wet wall as the site for the house's structural core and domestic interface. In her house, this usually minor element has been transformed into an unusual monolithic cast-in-place pink concrete wall. This pink wall crux supports a bivouacked lean-to style roof, stairs between levels, a nested bathroom, a suspended private wing, and a fireplace: all the necessary plumbing to live. The wall element functions like a Swiss Army knife to permit open plan living areas for the rest of the house that play formally and programmatically with the lodge house typology, incorporating broad, abstract geometric spatial delineations through color and material. A curving wall extends from the house interior and continues the geometric theme onto the site and gardens.

At the far end of the site, where Stockholder's pink monolithic wall ends, she nestles a ready-made house trailer under the roofline eaves. The camper, used as a bedroom, is incorporated into the house by stairway access through the pink wall. Structure and material are fused into one, balancing the house in a perpetual state of re-composition, the raw building material gels around standard appliances and fixtures. Stockholder's eclectic arrangement of materials and colors imbue her design with a painterly sensibility cast in space, with references and origins to domestic vernaculars, turned inside-out, juxtaposing a new program with traditional spatial patterns of social dwellings.

The house as a whole seeks to establish a new territory for cultural expansion and civic reclamation while assuring that, in the interim, each new outpost will contain all the ingredients for a self-sustaining microcosm.

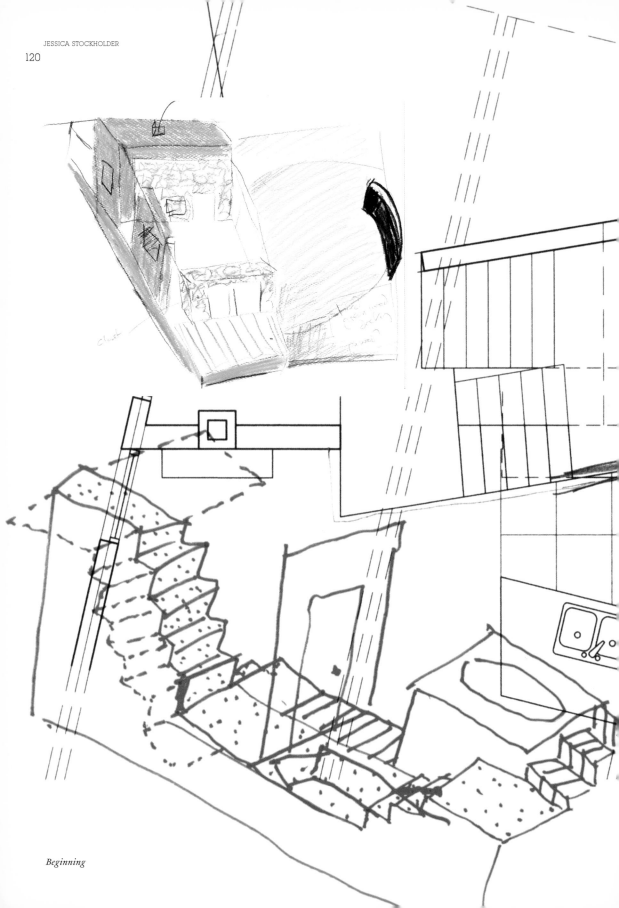

Beginning

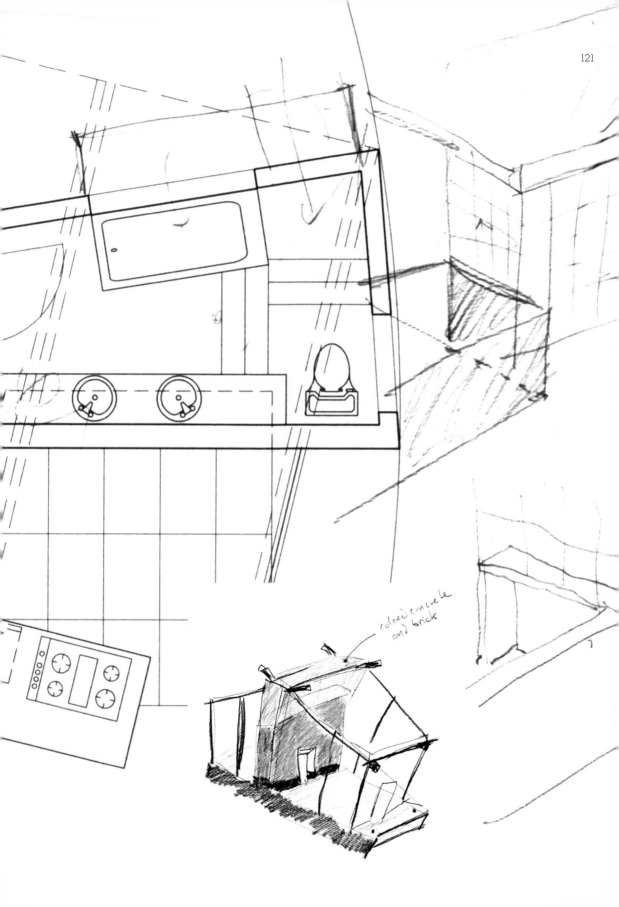

colored concrete
and brick

The house, then the garden (a demand for some kind of site). Developing pictorial moments.

door?

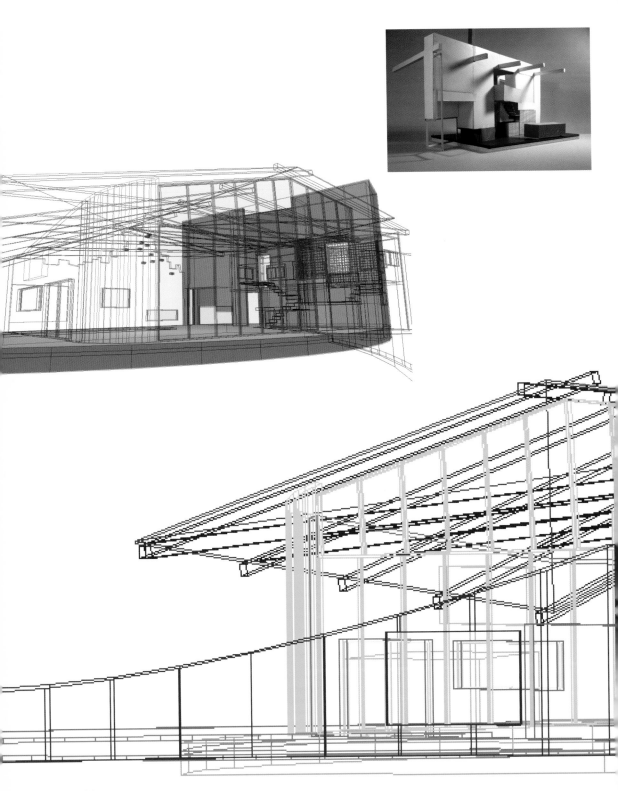

The how of the structure

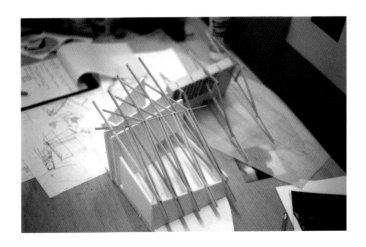

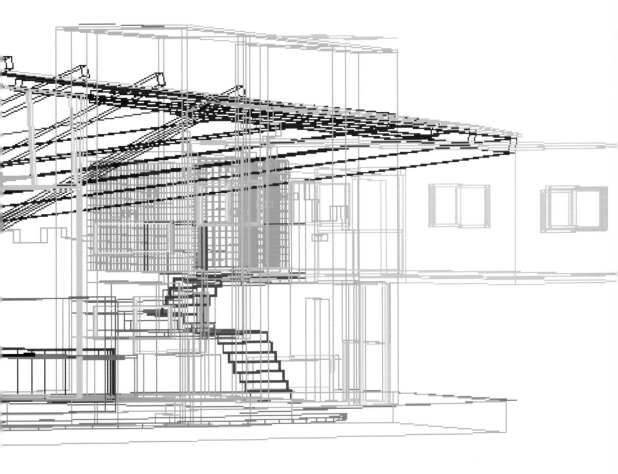

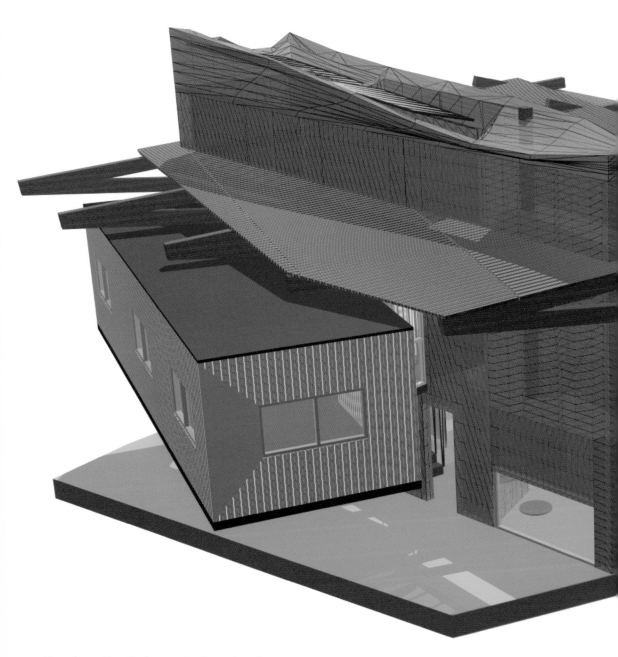

The roof as an object. The fragmented wall meets the roof.

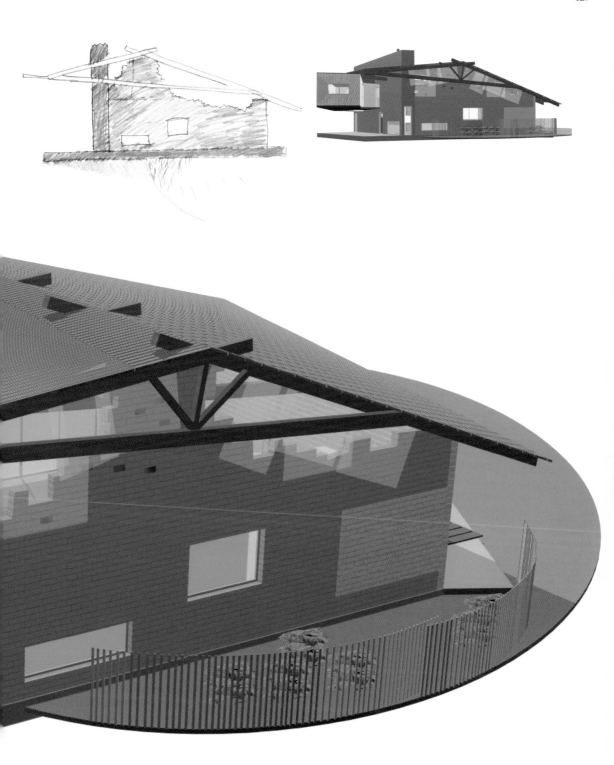

The glass wall and the purple concrete wall both function architecturally and pictorially

floorwire

When first approached by Alan and Linda to design a house without a site I thought it a peculiar problem, particularly for me. I specialize in making sculpture in response to particular sites. But it was an intriguing invitation; both Linda and Alan were so full of energy and open-minded, offering their energies and minds to serve my ideas. It was an irresistible invitation. And the result thus far is truly collaborative.

Though this house presently exists only as a group of illustrations of various kinds, and because this is the first time I have worked so intensely on something that exists only as a set of plans, I am impressed with how much is accomplished. I feel that this house could, and in some sense does, exist. However, I want to be clear that, if this house is built, the plans and ideas should evolve to be responsive to a particular site.

The first of anything is a very different experience than what follows. This is my first house, and I felt no confusion about what mattered to me. I thought to put together two of my favorite things: minimalist sculpture and West Coast architecture. Cool and warm contrasted. I love the immediacy of experience and call to the material world of minimalism; and I love the cult of the individual and the pointing at subjective mind space that is suggested by contemporary West Coast peaked roof houses.

The pink concrete base and center utility wall both speak of minimalist sculpture. I think of Donald Judd. The weight of the concrete and its plasticity are beautiful. Concrete—like the earth—is heavy, weighted, and pulls downward anchoring the house. In contrast, the timber structure that forms the peaked roof reaches upward creating inside the house a fiction of, or a mirror of, the sky outside. It creates a feeling of expansiveness and lightness tinged with the warmth of wood—the human touch associated with crafting wood and the "West Coast lifestyle."

The top of the concrete wall is slumped, breaking away from the control of the forms. The brick wall in the back (or is it the front?) of the house is incomplete, speaking of ruins and leaving room for the house to be many things at once. That this wall does not quite reach the roof also gives autonomy to the roof structure. The roof is an object placed over the walls. Light is let in between the wall and the roof. This is another kind of window.

Inside the house the color of the floor, the bricks and the pink concrete base resonate with the grass and the purple wall outside. The purple concrete wall winds its way from outside to inside. The color of the materials in the house and outside are of two natures. Some are surface colors and others are solid volumes running through the material. The colors at times sit still, solidly anchored to material and at various junctures they jump up and resonate across space with other colors as if they are not material in nature, jumping up to the retina. This duality of experience is always present in my work.

And there is the camper, lifted up and stuck to the pink concrete wall to provide a bedroom. And the kitchen cupboards faced with facings from pieces of baroque furniture. And the stair railing which makes use of a marlin surfboard. These prefab elements bring with them a sense of the wideness of the world. The aesthetic or order that my building proposes is knit into an ongoingness outside of it.

Space and volume

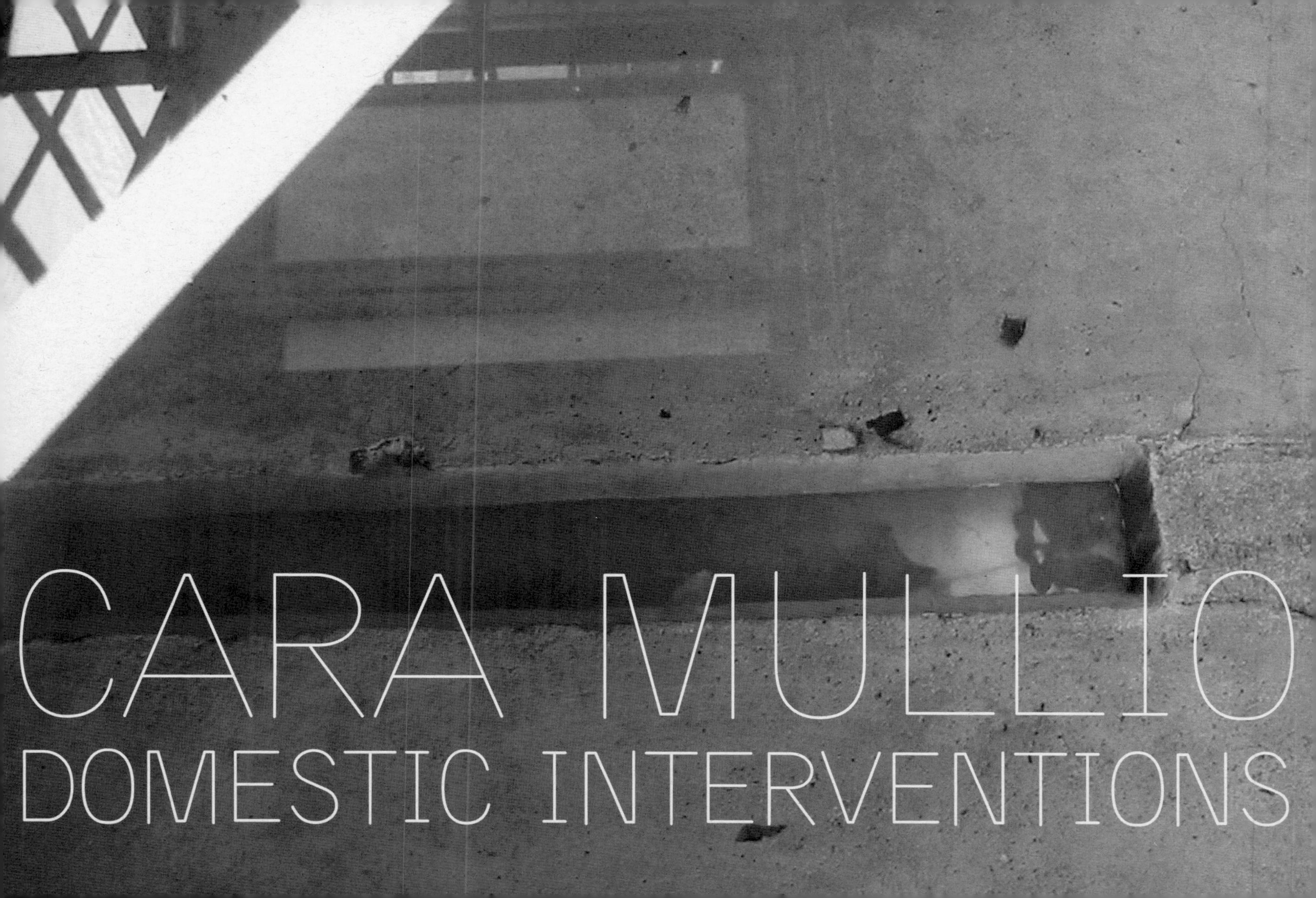
CARA MULLIO
DOMESTIC INTERVENTIONS

*Together let us desire, conceive, and create the new structure of the future,
which will embrace architecture and sculpture and painting in one unity.*
WALTER GROPIUS, 1919 [1]

...imagination augments the values of reality.
GASTON BACHELARD, 1969 [2]

Id(r)ealism

Should a domestic environment create and be responsible for its own subjective authority? Have spatial functions changed to accommodate current fluid social patterns? Why lapse into the conventional model of the house, when domestic relationships are changing? Unrestricted by external demands of program, scale, site condition, and finances, the selected artists Kevin Appel, Barbara Bloom, Chris Burden, Jim Isermann, T. Kelly Mason, Julian Opie, Renée Petropoulous, David Reed, and Jessica Stockholder have been invited to conceive new domestic forms that reinvestigate, reinvent, challenge and posit questions about the habitation of private space.

Through this unique set of circumstances, the artists, unconfined by architectural preconceptions and conventions, have had the freedom to think and invent the new house as a spatial and social entity. *TRESPASSING: Houses x Artists* was originally initiated by the New York-based architecture firm OpenOffice. A consortium of Principals with diverse backgrounds in both architecture and fine art, OpenOffice is committed to the pursuit of interdisciplinary collaborations that engage artist, architects, and inventors of new materials and technologies—used in a variety of ways—to create open-concept projects. The *TRESPASSING* projects represent the purest distillation of the firm's conceptual focus: nine contemporary artists each invited to co-design a house under optimal creative conditions. Over the course of a three-year venture, OpenOffice has acted as a creative partner, sustaining the articulation and output of the artistic and conceptual process of each project. Through a wide range of

architectural methods, including traditional modeling and drawing, computer animation, and other developing digital processes, OpenOffice has functioned as a collaborative facilitator, creating a climate in which the theoretical can be challenged, trespassed, and, in some cases, realized.

Over the course of this continuous collaborative investigation several key points in the discourse began to take precedence. First was the project's capacity to provide intensive opportunities for architectural research through the exploration of innovative developments in spatial concepts, building technologies, and architectural forms. Of equal importance was the fusing (at times colliding) relationship between architecture and the art practices, where moving in unknown territories produced fantastic results. This alliance has witnessed the emergence, articulation, and presentation of unique programs and house constructs that form a hybrid of the conceptual terrains claimed by disparate disciplines. Finally, raising the public's awareness of the role of architecture and design in day-to-day life is of paramount importance to this project and to the characters involved.

Architecturally I am satisfied—it is a thoroughbred and will either attract
people or repulse them... my fate is settled one way or the other.
RUDOLF SCHINDLER, LETTER TO THE GIBLINGS, KINGS ROAD HOUSE, 24 APRIL 1922 [3]

The Supreme Architectural Model for Living

The house is one of the most socially and politically potent architectural forms available and, as such, it has long been a testing ground for new building technologies and social paradigms. It is to the private dwelling that we attach our deepest aesthetic, psychological, and physiological impulses. As our species oldest experiment in environmental engineering, the house embodies the essence of subjective space. Through its function as our first universe, the house remains a highly resonant form and an ideal nexus for understanding the relationship of the human body to built space and, of course, serves the purest of requirements: the basic demand for shelter. [4]

The term "house" in the vernacular conception is too small to adequately define the *TRESPASSING* collaborative undertaking. House, as it is most commonly understood, is the fictive product of endless social, aesthetic, and commercial mediation. The linguistics of "house" has delimited the boundaries of exploration that have transpired, as readily seen in the majority of built domestic environments. This narrow definition of the house type continues to dominate contemporary language, that is unless, through rigorous experimentation, we can begin to expand and redefine our understanding of what the house can be and, in turn, to who we are becoming.

The diverse collection of house projects ventures beyond the traditional, almost static, term of what a house is and how it serves its occupants. As a formal construct, the domestic environment is nearly unparalleled in its sweeping popularity and is, in all of its forms, a basic necessity for all. The *TRES-*

PASSING exhibition draws on this broad recognition of the house by bringing together contemporary artists and the public—producers and user—in the exploration of new materials and ideas on the domestic environment. The idea of the house is studied in architectural, art, and domestic terms and in these projects it is brought into the public forum through the presentation of experimental media and highly interactive and hands-on experiences.

The scope of the project and installation lie far beyond the traditional museum presentations of art and architecture, instead delving into substantive interactions that engage the materiality of work on view. An open forum was provided to the artists and architects to establish the work as speculative concepts in a narrative framework. This critical liberty of the artists total conceptualization is reflected in part by the manner in which each idea is interactively articulated through a number of techniques, simulating the experience of material, scale, action and time in the gallery space.

R.M. Schindler's Kings Road House one of the venues for the exhibition, exists in a symbiotic relationship with the exhibited house constructs. By presenting the exhibition at a location that is, in and of itself, a domestic experiment, an ultimate and total landscape is created that reflect the philosophical underpinnings of both the *TRESPASSING* project and the nature of an architectural masterwork.

Built in 1921, the house became not only the abode for two couples but was also Schindler's primary workplace for more than three decades, providing

*I wasn't trying to make a big or precious statement about architecture or
trying to do an important work: I was trying to build a lot of ideas.*
FRANK GEHRY, GEHRY HOUSE, 1979 5

a long-term residence for the progressive articulation
of his architectural and social concerns. Schindler
referred to his house design as "a cooperative
dwelling" and the duality of the house as both
private residence and public meeting space
expresses Schindler's aspirations of communal living,
making the site a highly specific model of architectural practices and social commitments. His
pioneering residence is arguably the most crystal-
lized example of the monumental changes to the
programming of domestic space that lie at the heart
of the California modernist tradition and a perfect
stage-set for this exhibition on investigative living
explorations.

The Artists Responses

In every instance, the individuals sought to redefine
the notion of "house" and establish an inimitable
standard of residential design. Each project is valid,
first and foremost, as an idea, a conception of
human interaction with built space. The projects
were pulled from the labyrinth of the unconscious
and delivered into material space through a series
of architectural interventions. The creative discourse
represented by these projects covers questions of
typology and urbanism, explores the notions of
private and communal constructs, and addresses
living environments on a global scale. Many of the
projects explore the nurturing microcosm of the
house, while others reach outward to focus on the
macrocosmic notion of the house as a socially
inclusive open system.

A critical aspect of the *TRESPASSING* project has
been the testing of new ideas on a great scale and
inviting the experts of many fields to assist in the
discovery of new found ways of seeing space. Strict
realism did not enter into discussions unless it was
a central issue. Industry leaders from the fields of
digital animation and material manufacture helped
to provide new models for the visualization and
fabrication of these challenging and rigorous
constructs. It is the intention and hope of all involved
on the project that these new models will have
long-reaching applications throughout the practice
of architecture, art, and design.

In an early phase of process, several of the houses
were intended to be built as physical full-scale
mock-ups. As the projects became more concretized,
it was realized that bringing the projects to three-

dimensional arenas neither should not, nor could not be the primary objective. Traditionally, the three-dimensional realization of a project, often at the cost of the original conceptual thrust, is an architects' primary goal. However, with this project, the first duty was to the artists' conceptions, in all their detailed complexity. To this end, the focus turned to separating the commercial and physical constraints of the brick and mortar world from the imaginative play of pure design. As the project continued to evolve, the prerogative became a focus on the definitions, re-definitions, and re-adaptations of the house as a prototype for future living, in whatever form that may take.

The conceptual evolution of the projects and their chapter chronicling have served as a platform for experimentation and dialogue between the curator, artists, architects, and consultants. This conversation has extended the way architectural concepts potentially meet with developing tactics for rendering and building. The houses have also generated a series of concepts of domestic space that promise to amplify discussions within the discipline of architecture as well as within the general public about the nature, function, and form of the house.

House Projects

Each of the nine houses have been rendered and presented with an array of new media and this way of presentation changes the way an observer visualizes social spaces, therefore allowing a further examination of the impact of changing scales as a tool for constructing an account of each project. Due to the spatial complexities of the artists' presentations, each project accommodates a number of core issues that are dominant to differing degrees. Although each of the nine proposals explore a unique set of ideas of spaces, there is a visible transference of viewpoints that incorporate popular vernaculars, ideal utopias and living modes of house designs.

Several projects originated with the idea of an altered vernacular architecture. Isermann addresses this through a colorful folded plate roof and undulating ceiling forms that allow for a unique clerestory light condition. Much of his body of work explores domestic cues and signals. The textile motifs of his sculpture and installations bear signs of the suburban vernacular realized through a meticulous crafting of material. For *TRESPASSING*, Isermann expands his areas of concern to create a modular housing system, dictated by the flexible ceiling structure, that becomes the site for structural and spatial invention. Mason's house probes prefabricated interior spaces and building technology, creating rooms that are as detachable and flexible as furniture is normally considered. Mason's proposal involves the strategic adaptation of less costly construction processes, such as the Butler building—a pre-engineered metal building system. Stockholder employs the typical small-scale residential convention of a wet wall cast in place, painted pink, as the site for the house's structural core and domestic interface. Stockholder's house construct can be seen as an extrapolation from her installations. In her pink cast wall, one can recognize the authority of color that runs throughout her work. The residential cast wet wall is in line with Stockholder's adaptation of the familiar object to unfamiliar uses, creating opportunities for subversion, as objects are reconfigured to hold new functions.

Another theme considers the creation of private ideal utopic dwellings. Artifice and its manifestations are a central theme in Bloom's work. In Bloom's house construct, this artifice gives way to analogue. Here, Bloom questions the nature of domestic functionality through the production of a template that exists as an analogue to the physical house and maps how the inhabitant interacts with the house and landscape environs. Bloom's house moves from the witnessing of past navigation, explored in earlier work, to the tracking of memory in the moment in which it is made. The Burden house offers up a "small skyscraper" structure that evades Los Angeles building codes by keeping its spatial requirements to the letter, if not the spirit of the law—testing the codes and realizing rules are indeed meant to be challenged, not accepted. Reed posits the dwelling, and more specifically the bedroom, as the ideal environment for viewing art—an environment conducive to inductive rather than deductive logic. Using the language of the intimate domestic space, the Reed house creates an immersive environment in which the viewers' relationship with the apparatus of installation is on par with their responses to the art itself.

Finally the exhibition explores new perspectives on living. Appel's set of interconnecting pavilions unfolds into multiple gardens, extracting the painting canvas into spatial configurations. The pavilions employ structural glass, in various colors and opacities in an arrangement of vignettes to explore shifting degrees of private space. Appel's paintings have explored an abiding, if often critical interest in modernism, its promises and its discontents. In his offering for this exhibition, the extroversion of mid-century architecture gives way to a more nuanced understanding of the house as intrinsically private space. Another inclusion in this section is Opie's prefabricated building typology that can be constructed on a case by case basis. Opie's work has heretofore employed the use of traditional genres, such as the landscape, the portrait, the nude, the still life, etc. to create a kind of formal language. However, Opie's house represents a departure from his established oeuvre, as he creates a nested system of elements providing varying degrees of flexibility. Petropoulos explores new domestic relationships in a dwelling for an extended family or multiple families exploiting the model of the minimart/Stop & Go. By taking cues from this cultural phenomenon (seemingly indispensable in an American's life), the house adopts qualities that have led to the convenience store's widespread acceptance and feeling of need.

...build in imagination, unconcerned about technical difficulties.
The boon of imagination is always more important than all technique,
which always adapts itself to one's creative will.

WALTER GROPIUS, 1919 [6]

Final Thoughts

The *TRESPASSING* project represents a conceptual journey through an unprecedented collaborative enterprise. Throughout the dialoguing that transpired among artists, architects, curator, and consultants, parallels between the processes and practices of art and architecture have acted as cues to a new kind of work product that cannot be accurately defined by current critical frameworks. Though groundbreaking at first glance, the interrelationships between art and architecture, technology and academia that *TRESPASSING* fosters are part of a larger tradition. Indeed, they are the practices that form and inform both the Western art historical and architectural lineage. This form of collaborative play is central to the evolution of any of these respective fields.

Technological development has driven society toward an ever-increasing specialization of skills, which allows for wonderful opportunities. However, if pushed too far it produces less of a need for creative interactions. Therefore, this project balanced—pushed backward and forward simultaneously—a fine line of providing an applicable foundation for looking into the future but always acknowledging the authenticity of the artists' work and intentions.

At the beginning of the twenty-first century, culture stands at the brink of its technological threshold where there is a fluidity about information that cannot be contained. The meaning of meaning is in question. Through multidisciplinary experimentation, a new kind of highly adaptive syncretism begins to emerge. It is only through creating the forum for conciliance between practices that information can take on value.

Notes

1. Walter Gropius, *Programme of the Staatliche Bauhaus in Weimar* (April 1919). Four-page leaflet with a title-page woodcut by Lyonel Feininger and Gropius's Manifesto and Program. Reprinted in Hans M. Wingler, *The Bauhaus* (Cambridge, Mass., The MIT Press, 1978).

2. Gaston Bachelard, *The Poetics of Space*, translated Maria Jolas (Boston: Beacon Press, 1969).

3. Rudolf Schindler, letter to Sophie S. Gibling and Edmund J. Gibling, 24 April 1922, (Pauline Schindler Papers, Architecture and Design Collection, University Art Museum. University of California, Santa Barbara).

4. Gaston Bachelard, *The Poetics of Space*.

5. Germano Celant, *Frank Gehry: Buildings and Project* (New York: Rizzoli International Publications, 1985).

6. Walter Gropius, *New Ideas on Architecture* (April 1919). Four-page leaflet published on the occasion of an "Exhibition for Unknown Architects" with three manifesto-like texts by Walter Gropius, Bruno Taut, and Adolf Behne. Reprinted in Ulrich Conrads, *Programs and Manifestoes on 20th Century Architecture* (Cambridge, Mass., The MIT Press, 1997).

SPACE TO THINK.

THOUGHTS ON VISUALITY AND THE LIBERATION OF SPACE IN TRESPASSING

D. RIEHLE.

L.D.

To see a World in a Grain of Sand
And a Heaven in a Wild Flower
Hold Infinity in the palm of your hand
And eternity in an hour
WILLIAM BLAKE, *AUGURIES OF INNOCENCE*

Space in Two Dimensions

Our experience of three-dimensional space has been irrevocably transformed by contemporary visuality, which presents the sensate experience of other places and sites as pale replicas of their technologically-mediated representations. Embodied experience has become, consequently, largely unnevessary. insted point of view is everything. High-density TV, role-playing video games, digital cinema with auditorium seating, and the World Wide Web are consumed not as images that flatten real dimensionality, but as portals whose views claim a cultural authority derived from dynamic movement and varying perspective. The viewer holds still; it's what the portal reveals that keeps moving, keeps changing. Space is liberated from its reference to corporeality in a cultural shift that fortifies architecture's status as a paradigm through which to view the outside world. Given that this is the modern experience of space, then what does "home" mean anymore? The ocular framing presented by the television image or the computer screen modifies not only how we conceptualize our relation to the "outside" world. These viewing devices also replicate a defining feature of the bourgeois home: the window, the (in)visible boundary between exterior and interior spaces, the boundary that in fact brings these classifications into being. The snapshot of an anchorman on the precipice of the latest catastrophe; simultaneously viewed, multiple camera shots of a Hollywood event; video games that mimic first-person point of view; channel-surfing that casts each of us as flaneur wandering through post-urban, virtual landscapes— these visual technologies and their virtual perspectives illusively mimic the dynamic, real-time

experience of the window. Through these windows, flashes of reality appear almost hyper-real. We are presented with views of a world that can be mastered because it is visible and of a private, interior self as precisely that which defies voyeuristic access. By performing the prospects with which we install ourselves, contemporary visuality conflates two versions of the home: its site-specificity as a perspectival coordinate that locally and globally locates us, and its ideological power as a metaphor for the values invested in that location. Material, geographical, and abstract notions of home merge with visuality as their shared means of enactment.

By inviting nine visual artists to conceptualize a "house," *TRESPASSING: Houses x Artists* invokes this visual mediation of domestic space. One consequence of the collaboration has been to "make new" the ocular relationships that position the home's inhabitant(s) as inside to the house's outside—in here among "us" versus out there among the world at large and protected by privacy against public display and observation. Harvesting the artist's distinctive conception of the mobility of visual languages, *TRESPASSING* denaturalizes the visual codes by which an inhabitant socially installs himself at "home" and raises several questions about the body's exclusion from these visual codes by mass media. Not the least of these is the problem of what role the body can play in our predominantly visual experience of cultural and architectonic space.

Imaginary Inhabitation

How does one inhabit a house that hasn't been built yet? Architects continually confront this question when dealing with the demands of clients; inversely, all of us repetitively view spaces that do not require bodily inhabitation to qualify as spatial. Faux domestic set-ups in stores like Restoration Hardware and Pottery Barn, storefronts designed to replicate living rooms, and TV/magazine publicity displaying celebrity décor—all function as virtual windows into virtual spaces. They substitute the imaginative projection into represented spaces for the corporeal occupation of actual ones. The home is everywhere but becomes a no-where, a non-place, a recurrent visual simulation.

TRESPASSING responds to this architectural conundrum of artifice by collapsing the distinction between visual consumption and the embodied consumption of space. Context in this regard is crucial. We set foot into a privately-endowed architectural monument and public gallery, like the Bellevue Art Museum (Seattle) or the Schindler House (itself a home remade into an exhibition space) and enter an exhibition of built structures, photographs, drawings and designs, moving images, mock-ups, furniture, and models created in collaboration with visual artists. We peer through the miniature windows of Kevin Appel's model glass structure; we inspect the temporal narrative implied by David Reed's process model; we handle the concrete texture of Julian Opie's domestic sub-unit. Each method of representation suggests a different ideal of occupation— visual, nostalgic, temporal, or tactile—in order to inhabit the house that it signifies. Like Alice's during her adventures, the body is vari-

ously resized, repositioned, and relocated by different visual situations.

While we usually think of vision as a function performed by the body, *TRESPASSING* positions the body as a function performed by perception. The exhibition moves us deeper into the miniaturized worlds of architectural models, which can be consumed entirely while standing still. As such, the small-scale model is a "house within a house": an enclosed domestic space within an enclosed domestic space that presents interiority as a narrative of infinite regress. As a consequence, "it represents the *tension* between inner and outer spheres, between exteriority and interiority." [1] Elsewhere the exhibition shrinks our perspective by confronting us with larger or even life-size architectural replicas that, like the Schindler House itself, are impossible to view in a single glance. Drawings and axonometric designs, meanwhile, present the house as an object to be perceived and dissected with the creator's God-like, disembodied authority. Alternatively, moving images and serialized photographs play with the strained epistemological relationship between space, time, and memory—the interpretive uncertainty evoked by space's dependence upon time. These flashes of light and image literalize the negative presence of space (by definition the absence of thing-ness) as an experiential by-product of temporal narrative or as the assembled memory of discrete views. These architectural renderings are not unlike one of Eadweard Muybridge's groundbreaking photographic series: they demonstrate that the animal's locomotion through space is only an optical illusion. [2]

As visual shaman well practiced in the magic of the eye, artists appreciate this—that space is an optical illusion, a visual effect of the modern body's craving for coherence, control, and history. Some *TRESPASSING* projects tease this craving, others present it as the fore-pleasure to endless desire. In Appel's model, each moment's view exists in isolation from other moments. A spot in time determined by situation rather than memory, each sight thereby liberates the viewer from modernity's nostalgic longing for continuity. Barbara Bloom's house purposefully unravels the overdetermined conflation of objects, identity, and biographical memory that limits the phantasmagoric possibilities of space to linear narrative. The fixed functions that conventionally organize domestic space are transformed into self-conscious aesthetic and positional choices in T. Kelly Mason's and Opie's modular designs. Chris Burden's mini-skyscraper mocks institutional intervention in the location and construction of private space by literalizing the prescriptive requirements of its post-industrial site. Renée Petropolous's house interrogates the spatial conventions that oppose private individualism to social interaction and domestic activities to modern communal rituals. David Reed's design resists the reification of vision and therefore identity by presenting enclosure as a process of infinite expansion. The mock-ups of Jim Isermann's clerestory ceiling and Jessica Stockholder's anti-house materialize the dislocations built into the home's dual role as aesthetic experience and functional residence.

These various representations of the house aim to destabilize one of the major disparities upon which domestic architecture is based, the difference between enclosure and exclusion.

"The home is a mechanism for classification," writes Beatriz Colomina. "It collects views and, in doing so, classifies them."[3] In the modern house, traditional classifications are naturalized by functionality: the office, kitchen, bathroom, master bedroom, and kids' rooms allocate space according to the premise that we should not work, prepare food, expel waste, play children's games, and have sex in the same room, for example, or under the same set of eyes. These classifications also enforce the distribution of power among family members by determining who is included in or excluded from certain domains or during particular activities. In this respect, OpenOffice's invitation to artists to imagine a house is an attempt to re-imagine the basic social unit, the nuclear family, long sanctified by the Western tradition of domestic withdrawal from the public gaze. The subsequent houses liberate vision by erasing or restyling the boundaries that police it, and they show how domestic living can be re-imagined only to the degree that it relinquishes its propagation of differences.[4]

Vanishing Points

This re-imagination of domestic representation and, in turn, of its divisive mechanisms of normative visuality also suggests certain more ominous side effects to our current linkage of space and ocularity. Not least among these are the implications of the depreciation of separate spheres. The division of space into private and public domains (and, in turn, into neighborhoods) has long been the basis for social classifications of gender, race, sexuality, and class. The home is feminine, the professional suite is masculine, and the difference between a renovated Schindler building in West Hollywood and a dilapidated Schindler building in Compton is determined as much by ethnicity and economics as by geographical convenience. Allowing this much, then the increasing invasion of private space by public view—inaugurated with modernist architecture and reinvigorated by its late twentieth-century renaissance—conserves the distribution of power established during Reagan's glory years. In spite (or because) of postmodernism, a liberalist illusion of democracy continues to prevail.

Allowing that *TRESPASSING* generates a sense of the body as one site among many, then that body's classification is contingent upon the views framed by/for it. One effect is that, like "home" itself, the body operates only metaphorically, an architectonic figure positioned by representation and perception. Although often hailed as a liberating development, from another perspective the subsequent diminution of the division between "in here" (private) and "out there" (public) naturalizes the colonization of one by the other. It is no accident, for example, that this development in the ideology of space, and the space of the body, coincides with corporate globalization. We work harder, longer, around the clock, and in our homes. What we buy, read, e-mail, and watch becomes information available for public view. We relocate ourselves to a social space on the cusp of this separation—the cinema, for example—and discover ourselves hounded by corporate sponsorship in even its most intimate corners. Gradually, our notions of individual subjectivity and its "housing" by the body shift in response. Our most intimate spaces—like our "inner" thoughts and feelings—are de-privatized so that we greet the corporate flux of desire, exchange, and substitution not as a temporary houseguest but as a member of the family.[5] Perhaps, then, we should be more alert to the representational shifts that signal a revolution in the body's experience of home.

TRESPASSING presents an incisive intervention in this collision of spatial experience and ocular signs. As a sustained encounter between experiences of domestic space and mechanisms of visuality, it creates a new space at the boundary between public consumption and private reverie. Like all uncategorizable spaces, it embodies the paradox of heterotopia.[6] It is utopic and inclusive of a range of representational possibilities for the "dream house"; simultaneously, it is atopic and exclusive, in that these representations are necessarily excluded from broader public discourse by their containment in this place. Only positioned as a location between these two spaces can *TRESPASSING* expose the shadows at the edges of our dreams.

146

Notes

1. Susan Stewart, *On Longing: Narratives of the Miniature, the Gigantic, the Souvenir, the Collection* (Durham, N.C., and London: Duke University Press, 1993), 61; my emphasis.

2. Anthony Vidler, "Space, Time, and Movement," in *At the End of the Century: One Hundred Years of Architecture*, Richard Koshalek and Elizabeth A.T. Smith (Los Angeles: The Museum of Contemporary Art, Los Angeles, and New York: Harry N. Abrams, 1998), 105–6.

3. Beatriz Colomina, "The Split Wall: Domestic Voyeurism," in *Sexuality and Space*, ed. Colomina (Princeton, N.J.: Princeton Papers on Architecture, 1992), 113.

4. Like inside/outside, interiority/exteriority, subjectivity/object-hood, privacy/publicity, then/now.

5. A case in point: "Homeland Security" a phrase that overwrites the particular place-ness of "home" with the patriarchal authority of a transnational Father.

6. Michel Foucault, "Of Other Places," 1997, *Documenta X*, repr. *Diacritics* 16, no. 1 (September 1986).

ACKNOWLEDGMENTS
ARTISTS BIOS

148

Acknowledgments

First and foremost we wish to thank the nine participating artists in *TRESPASSING: Houses x Artists* for engaging in an exploration of unique and visionary house projects and venturing into uncharted territories in the realization of new forms. In the course of a four-year investigation it has been a true pleasure to work in parallel with Kevin Appel, Barbara Bloom, Chris Burden, Jim Isermann, T. Kelly Mason, Julian Opie, Renée Petropoulos, David Reed, and Jessica Stockholder and watch new doors open for all that have participated in realizing this project. We would like to expressly thank Stan Douglas, Peter Halley, and Charles Ray for being part of the opening dialogue of the exhibition, generously contributing their time to thinking about the house. We also wish to extend a special thank you to Rodney Hill, Creative Consultant, for providing insight in helping to establish the poetic framework and grounds for developing this ambitious project. We are indebted to the insight that Leilani D. Riehle has provided since the beginning of the project, which she has encapsulated in her perceptive catalogue essay.

Extraordinary thanks to OpenOffice partners Lyn Rice and Galia Solomonoff, whose intellectual support and trust on the project made it possible. With admiration, we thank all the interns and consultants in our office that have contributed extra time and effort, including Julian deSmedt, Cornelia Fischer, Christina Forrer, Henry Gunawan, Martin Hagel, Leif Halverson, Damen Hamilton, Jay Hindmarsh, Astrid Lipka, Cristian Mare, Alina Taalman, and Kathy Tsina. Special thanks to interns David Brooks, Krystal Chang, and Michael Vahrenwald, and to the Cooper Union Career Services staff, Melissa Benca, Cathy Carrington, and Narisa Svetvilas. Thanks to Kevin Farnham and Method designers Thomas

Noller, April Starr, Chris Torrens, and to all the Method team for donating their expertise in creating the elegantly devised original Web site. Additional thanks to Monte Bartlett and Fonte PR in presenting the Web site to the public and thank you to Ove Arup, Matt King, and Nigel Tonks, for their assistance in considering issues of engineering. Thank you to all the artists' galleries for their assistance and early encouragement of the project.

Thank you to those who have lent their invaluable expertise, time, and materials to the fabrication of the elements of the projects realized for exhibition purposes including Adam Wheeler, Gaston Nogues, Colby Mayes, Stephen Traeger, Jane Hart from Lemon Sky Projects and Editions, Joseph Hutchins & Co., Inc., Tony Giammarinaro and Nick Mango at Atlantic Industrial Technologies, Bosch Aluminum Structural Framing, and Greneker Urethane Technologies. Special thanks to Yale architecture students Ben Griswold, Keilem Ng, Siobahn Reynders, Ben Rosenblum, and the Yale School of Architecture Shop in the making of Jessica Stockholder's exhibition model.

On the MAK Center staff we thank, Gamynne Guillotte, Project Coordinator, for her tenacious spirit and smart ability to take on a project of this detailed magnitude; LouAnne Greenwald, Deputy Director, for her conscientious drive and co-support in realizing the Center's creative dreams; Angelica Fuentes, Bookkeeper, in managing all of the financial demands; Bob Sweeney for providing us with his knowledge and allowing us to play with the supreme example of domestic environment, the Kings Road House. True thanks to Michael Worthington, designer, in creating an extension of the exhibition that is equally intriguing and aesthetically multidimensional; and to Stephanie Emerson, for her direction and expertise in catalogue editing and incorporating the many voices of this publication.

The staff and Trustees of Bellevue Art Museum (BAM) deserve great credit for forming this significant collaboration with the MAK Center. By making this major organizational and financial commitment, they proclaimed their strong belief in the project's importance.

BAM's Exhibitions and Education Program Fund contributed to this exhibition. Sustained Museum support comes from the Corporate Council for the Arts/Arts Fund, King County Arts Commission Hotel/Motel Tax Revenues, Washington State Arts Commission, Bellevue Arts Commission, Standing Ovation, and BAM members and annual fund donors.

In addition to those intimately involved with the project, there were many people we would like to acknowledge whose advice, guidance, and help along the way proved invaluable. A very special thanks goes to Cecilia Maria Anderssen, Knut Asdam, Rosetta Brooks, Neil Denari, Frank Gehry, David and Lindsay Shapiro, Jonathan Steinke, John Sullivan, and Anne Walsh.

Thanks to Vito Acconci, Kevin Bone, Sophia Gruzdys, Robert Gunderman, Tanja Jordan, Ric Scofidio, Anita Thacher, and Roger White, who acted as advisors throughout the project's development, and to Robert Irwin for many insightful thoughts. Thanks also to Paola Antonelli, Art in General, Aaron Betsky, Mary Ellen Carol, Kimberlee Colin, Lynne Cooke, Marc

Foxx, Jay Gorney, Michael Govan, Claudia Gould, Peter Heimer, Betty Sue Hertz and Mary Ceruti, Edelbert Köb, David McAuliffe, Christine Nichols, Anne Pasternack, Mark Petr, Rolfe Ricke, Jim Schaeufele, Darcy Steinke, David Thorpe, Irene Tsatsos and Julie Deamer from Los Angeles Contemporary Exhibitions, Ola Wedebrunn, Heidi Zuckerman, and David Zwirner. Special thanks to the Greig Family Foundation for supporting *TRESPASSING: Houses x Artists* when it needed it most.

Special and sincere thanks to the funders and sponsors of *TRESPASSING: Houses x Artists*, including the Federal Chancellery, Department of the Arts and Federal Ministry of Education, Science and Culture of the Republic of Austria; the National Endowment for the Arts; the City of Los Angeles, Cultural Affairs Department; City of West Hollywood; the LLWW Foundation, and the New York Foundation for the Arts.

Finally we'd like to thank our families for giving unwaivering encouragement and inspiration.

Cara Mullio, Curator
Linda Taalman and Alan Koch, OpenOffice
Kathleen Harleman, Director, Bellevue Art Museum
Peter Noever, C.E.O. and Artistic Director, MAK Vienna

Biographies

Kevin Appel

Kevin Appel was born in Los Angeles in 1967. He received his B.F.A. from Parsons School of Design, New York, in 1990 and his M.F.A. from the University of California, Los Angeles, in 1995. He has had solo exhibitions at Marianne Boesky Gallery, New York, The Museum of Contemporary Art, Los Angeles, and Angles Gallery, Santa Monica, California. Recent exhibitions include "010101: Art in Technological Times" (San Francisco Museum of Modern Art, San Francisco, 2001); "Against Design" (Museum of Contemporary Art, San Diego, La Jolla, California, 2001); "Paintings at the Edge of the World" (Walker Art Center, Minneapolis, Minnesota, 2001); "Farve Volumen/Color Volume" (Kunsthalle Brandts Klaadefabrik, DK-Odense, Denmark, 1999); "DRIVE-BY: New Art from L.A." (South London Gallery, New York, 1999); "The Perfect Life: Artifice in L.A. 1999" (Duke University Museum of Art, Durham, North Carolina, 1999); "Abstract Painting Once Removed" (Contemporary Arts Museum, Houston, 1998); "Painting From Another Planet" (Deitch Projects, New York, 1998); "Inhabited Spaces: Artists Depictions" (Long Beach Museum of Art, Long Beach, California, 1997); "In Touch With..." (Galerie + Edition Renate Schröder, Cologne, Germany, 1997). In 1999, he was the recipient of the Citibank Emerging Artist Award at MOCA. Appel lives and works in Los Angeles.

Barbara Bloom

Barbara Bloom was born in 1951 in Los Angeles and received her B.F.A. from California Institute of the Arts in 1972. Selected solo exhibitions include, "Broken" (Gorney Bravin + Lee, New York, 2001); "A Birthday Party for Everything" (Susan Inglett/I. C. Editions, New York, 1999); "The Collections of Barbara Bloom" (Wexner Center for the Arts, Columbus, Ohio, 1998); "Pictures from the Floating World" (Sala de Exposiciones Rekalde, Bilbao, Spain, 1998); "Just Past" (The Museum of Contemporary Art, Los Angeles, 1996); "The Tip of the Iceberg" (Jay Gorney Modern Art, New York, 1991); and "The Reign of Narcissism" (Serpentine Gallery, London, 1990). She was the recipient of the Frederick Weisman Foundation Award (1991), the Louis Comfort Tiffany Foundation Award (1989), and the Due Mille Prize at the Venice Biennale (1988). Publications include, *Broken, with Abbott Miller* (New York: Pentagon, 2001); *The Gaze* (Parrish Art Museum, Southhampton, New York, 2000); *Vladimir Nabokov* (New York: Glenn Horowitz Bookseller, 1999); *The Passions of: Natasha, Nokiko, Nicola, Nanette and Norma* (Ostfildern, Germany: Hatje Cantz, 1993); *Never Odd Or Even* (Munich, Germany: Verlag Silke Schreiber, and Pittsburgh, Pennsylvania: The Carnegie Museum of Art, 1992); *The Reign of Narcissism: Guide Book* (Stuttgart: Würtem-bergischer Kunstverein; London: Serpentine Gallery; and Zurich: Kunsthalle Zürich, 1990). Bloom currently works and lives in New York.

Chris Burden

Chris Burden was born in Boston in 1946. He
obtained a B.F.A at Pomona College, Claremont,
California, in 1969 and an M.F.A at the University
of California, Los Angeles, in 1971. Burden has
exhibited and performed at numerous institutions
including the Museum of Conceptual Art, San
Francisco; the Institute of Contemporary Art, Boston;
The Museum of Modern Art, New York; the Centre
Georges Pompidou, Paris; the Whitney Museum
of American Art, New York; and the MAK, Vienna.
A retrospective of his work, "Chris Burden: A Twenty
Year Survey," was organized in 1988 by the Newport
Harbor Art Museum, Newport Beach, California.
In 1999, Burden exhibited at the 48th Venice Biennale
and the Tate Gallery in London. Burden currently
lives and works in California and teaches at the
University of California, Los Angeles.

Jim Isermann

Jim Isermann was born in 1955 in Kenosha, Wisconsin,
and received his B.F.A from the University of Wisconsin,
Milwaukee, in 1977 and his M.F.A. from the California
Institute of the Arts, Valencia, California, in 1980. Recent
solo exhibitions include, Richard Telles Fine Art (Los
Angeles, 2001); "Logic Rules" (The RISD Museum,
Providence, Rhode Island, 2000); "Vega" (Le
Magasin—Centre d'art Contemporain, Grenoble,
France, 1999); "Fifteen: Jim Isermann Survey, Institute
of Visual Arts" (University of Wisconsin, Milwaukee,
Wisconsin, 1998–99); "Herringbone + Houndstooth"
(Richard Telles Fine Art, Los Angeles, 1998);
"Cubeweave" (Feature Inc, New York, 1996); "Jim
Isermann/Jorge Pardo" (Richard Telles Fine Art,
Los Angeles, 1996); "Ynglingagatan 1" (Stockholm,
Sweden, 1995); and "Handiwork" (Feature Inc, New
York, 1994). His work has been featured in *Artforum*,
Art & Design, *Art issues*, *Art in America*, *Los Angeles
Times*, and the *New York Times*. He received a
Guggenheim Foundation Grant in 2001, the J. Paul
Getty Fellowship for the Visual Arts in 1999, and
a Visual Artist's Fellowship in Painting from the
National Endowment for the Arts in 1987.

T. Kelly Mason

T. Kelly Mason was born in Hollywood, California, in 1964. He received his B.A. from California State University at Long Beach in 1988 and his M.F.A. from Art Center College of Design, Pasadena, California, in 1990. Recent solo exhibitions include, "You Should've Been There" (Catherine Bastide/123 ASBL, Brussels, 2000); "Suggesting Islands, Stones, Water..." (Marc Foxx Gallery, Los Angeles, 1999); "Mid Winter Drawings" (Marc Foxx Gallery, Santa Monica, California, 1997); and "High Points Drifter" (Marc Foxx Gallery, Santa Monica, California, 1995). Recent group exhibitions include, "Made in Los Angeles" (Los Angeles County Museum of Art, Los Angeles, 2000); and "A Living Theater" (Salzburg Kunstverein, Salzburg, Austria, 1999). Mason has also presented music, events, and performances including, "The Future that Almost Wasn't" a collaboration with Diana Thater (Marshall Theater, Munich, Germany, 2000) and "Sampler 2" as part of "Sunshine and Noir: Art in Los Angeles, 1960–1997" (Louisiana Museum of Modern Art, Humlebaek, Denmark, 1997). Mason was the recipient of a fellowship through Art Matters Inc., and his writings have appeared in *X-tra, Paradex, Transcript,* and *Spring Journal.* Mason lives and works in Los Angeles.

Julian Opie

Julian Opie was born in London in 1958. He attended Goldsmith's School of Art, London, from 1979 until 1982. Recent solo exhibitions include, the Wetterling Gallery, Stockholm (2001–2002); Ikon Gallery, Birmingham (2001), Lisson Gallery, London (2001); Abbaye saint Andre, centre d'Art Contemporain, Meymac, France (2000); Lenbachhaus Stadtische Galerie, Munich (1999); Primo Piano, Rome (1999); "Imagine you are moving" (Commissioned and Funded by BAA Plc, Heathrow Airport, London, 1998); Kunsthandlung H. Krobath & B. Wimmer, Vienna (1997); Gallery Nova Sin, Prague (1997); Gallery Analix Polla, Geneva (1996); "Paysages" (Le Channel, Galerie de l'Ancienne Poste, Calais, Monica De Cardenas, Milan, 1995). He was the recipient of the Sargant Fellowship at The British School in Rome (1995) and a residency at the Atelier Calder in Saché, France (1995–96), and was awarded Best Illustration for "Best of Blur" album at Music Week CADS (2001). Opie's work appears in numerous public collections including the Tate Gallery, London; the Stedelijk Museum, Amsterdam; the Museo d'Arte Contemporanea Prato; the Wadsworth Atheneum; the Arts Council of Great Britain; and the Israel Museum, Jerusalem. Opie lives and works in London.

Renée Petropoulos

Renée Petropoulos was born in Los Angeles. She received a B.A. in 1974, an M.A. in 1977, and an M.F.A. in 1979, all from the University of California, Los Angeles. Recent solo exhibitions include, "Having a Wonderful Time, West Pavilion, Art After 1800" (J. Paul Getty Museum, Los Angeles, 2000); "Drawings and Photographs/Douglas Station: Grant Mudford/ Renée Petropoulos" (Rosamund Felsen Gallery, Santa Monica, California, 1998); "Show Us Their Faces, Tell Us What They Said" (Rosamund Felsen Gallery, Santa Monica, California, 1995); "In memory of: In hope of" (Rosamund Felsen Gallery, Los Angeles, 1993); and "The Chicken or the Egg" (Rosamund Felsen Gallery, Los Angeles, 1991). She has been the recipient of the Ford Foundation Travel Fellowship, the Djerassi Foundation Fellowship, the California Arts Council Fellowship Grant, and the Art Matters Inc. Grant. Petropoulos lives in Venice, California.

David Reed

David Reed was born in San Diego, California, in 1946. He studied at the New York Studio School and the Skowhegan School of Painting and Sculpture in Maine and received a B.A from Reed College, Portland, Oregon, in 1968. Recent solo exhibitions include, "David Reed—You look good in blue" (St. Gallen Kunstmuseum, St. Gallen, Switzerland, 2001); "David Reed Painting/Vampire Study Center: Is Looking at an Abstract Painting Similar to a Vampire's not Reflecting in a Mirror?" (Goldie Paley Gallery, Moore College of Art and Design, Philadelphia and Corollary Research Station. Rosenbach Museum & Library, Philadelphia, 1999); "David Reed Paintings: Motion Pictures" (Museum of Contemporary Art, San Diego, California, 1998); "New Paintings for the Mirror Room and Archive in a Studio off the Courtyard" (Neue Galerie am Landesmuseum Joanneum, Graz, Austria, 1996); and "David Reed" (Kölnischer Kunstverein, Cologne, Germany, 1995). Publications include *David Reed Painting/Vampire Study Center: Is Looking at an Abstract Painting Similar to a Vampire's not Reflecting in a Mirror?* (Philadelphia: Goldie Paley Gallery, Moore College of Art and Design, 1999); *David Reed Paintings: Motion Pictures* (San Diego, California: Museum of Contemporary Art, 1998); *New Paintings for the Mirror Room and Archive in a Studio off the Courtyard by David Reed* (Graz, Austria: Neue Galerie am Landesmuseum Joanneum, 1996); *David Reed* (Cologne, Germany: Kölnischer Kunstverein, 1995). Reed lives and works in New York.

Jessica Stockholder

Jessica Stockholder was born in Seattle, Washington, in 1959. She received her B.F.A. from the University of Victoria, Victoria, British Columbia, Canada, in 1982 and her M.F.A. from Yale University in 1985. Recent solo exhibitions include "Vortex in the Play of Theatre with the Real Passion (for Kay Stockholder)" (Kunstmuseum St. Gallen, St. Gallen, Switzerland, 2000); "First Cousin Once Removed or Cinema of Brushing Skin" (The Power Plant, Toronto, Canada, 1999); "Torque, Jelly Role, and Goose Bump" (Musée Picasso d'Antibes, Antibes, France, 1998); "Nit Picking Trumpets of Iced Blue Vagueries" (Musée des Beaux-Arts de Nantes/La Salle Blanche, Nantes, France, 1998); "Your Skin in this Weather Bourne Eye-Threads & Swollen Perfume" (Dia Center for the Arts, New York, 1995). Selected recent publications include, *Jessica Stockholder: Vortex in the Play of Theatre with the Real Passion (for Kay Stockholder)*, 2001; *Jessica Stockholder: First Cousin Once Removed or Cinema of Brushing Skin*, 2000; and *Jessica Stockholder: Your Skin in this Weather Bourne Eye-Threads & Swollen Perfume*, 1996). She has been the recipient of the John Solomon Guggenheim Fellowship Award (Visual Art), the Canada Council "A" and "B" Grants, the National Endowment for the Arts Grant in Sculpture, and the First Alternate, Prix de Rome, American Academy of Rome. Stockholder currently lives and works in New Haven, Connecticut.

OpenOffice

Based in New York City, OpenOffice, currently directed by Alan Koch, Lyn Rice, Galia Solomonoff, and Linda Taalman, is a platform for art and architecture projects. The name declares the organization's commitment to a design process of open exchange. Collaborations with artists, designers, innovators, and specialists—invited on a project-by-project basis—merge diverse disciplines and stimulate conceptual investigation in an ongoing creative dialogue. Projects range from museums and other public buildings, exhibitions, public art installations, and master planning, to curatorial and content development, retail branding/prototyping, offices, and private houses. OpenOffice pursues urban and land-use planning techniques, as well as new materials and product research and development, as active elements in architectural practice. Recent projects include Dia: Beacon, Beacon, New York (1999–2003), a 292,000 square-foot museum and accompanying programs designed in collaboration with Robert Irwin, comprising a renovation of a 1929 industrial building and new additions for the Dia Center for Arts permanent collection; Public Art & Exhibition Master Plan for Ft. Lauderdale-Hollywood International Airport, Ft. Lauderdale, Florida (2001), with Public Art installations by Liam Gillick, Miles Coolidge, and Peter Kogler; Shiseido Cosmetics Counter Prototype in collaboration with Diller + Scofidio (2001–2002); and NhEW PAD (2001), a design for a nomadic, internet-order, multi-climate shelter prototype, in collaboration with COPENHAGEN-OFFICE, DK. OpenOffice has been recognized by The Architectural League of New York as one of the 2002 Emerging Voices in contemporary architectural practice. OpenOffice's work has been exhibited at numerous cultural institutions including the Berkeley Art Museum, New Museum, and the Vitra Design Museum.

Photography Credits

Courtesy of Angles Gallery, 21 top left; courtesy of Feature
Inc, 21 center; courtesy of Rosamund Felson Gallery, 21
bottom left; courtesy of Gagosian Gallery, 21 bottom center;
courtesy of Gorney, Bravin + Lee, 21 top center, bottom right,
39 top and bottom, 40 top, 42 bottom, 43 top and center,
120, 121, 122, 123 middle, 127 top left; courtesy of the
Solomon R. Guggenheim Museum, 108 top, 109; courtesy of
Robert Irwin, 10; courtesy of Grant Mudford, 108 bottom;
courtesy of Lisson Gallery, 21 center right; courtesy of Max
Protech Gallery, 21 top right; courtesy of the University of
California, Santa Barbara, Architectural Drawing Collection,
108 center, 114; courtesy of Michael Worthington, 133, 141,
147. All other photographs appear courtesy of the artists and
OpenOffice.